The Key

Denise Martinez Rossini

Tecassia
PUBLISHING

Published in 2020 by

Tecassia Publishing
Building 31186,
PO Box 6945,
London,
W1A 6US
www.tecassia.com

ISBN

Paperback 978-1-913916-00-8

Also available as an e-book 978-1-913916-01-5

Designed by Camilla Fellas Arnold

Dedication

To the magic in my life Christine and Terence,
my amazing children.

And to all you dancers under the stars who
believe in the magic of the universe.

Table of Contents

Author's Note

How this book came about was magical in its own right. It was guided to me in an instantaneous moment. I saw the book cover and title and knew I was to share my knowledge of the universe and all its wonderful gifts.

I wanted to share that everyone has magic within them and no matter what your background story is you can truly shine if you allow yourself to do so. We all have the right to live in love, joy and abundance.

I hope that this book will give you the tools to grow both your gifts and your light so you can achieve the life of your dreams.

Enjoy!

ACKNOWLEDGEMENTS

A massive thank you to my publisher Camilla Fellas Arnold. It was magic that brought us together through the law of attraction. I love how you can envision exactly what I have in mind and turn it into a thing of beauty. Thank you for your patience and encouragement in bringing *The Key* into reality.

Thank you to Jo my amazing virtual assistant and now dear friend. You bring easy order to my sometimes chaotic schedule. I couldn't get through my days without you!

Thank you to my sparkly friends the LOA twins. It's always a joy to work with you and share the magic on our journey.

My beautiful friend Cathlene Miner, thank you for our chats across the ocean. You are a true inspiration for so many women around the world, especially with your charity work for hopeful handbags.

Thank you, Marianne Jones, for your beautiful prayer circle – a place to find serenity and listen to your magical voice.

My amazing friend Leona Burton – thank you for all your encouragement on my journey and your wicked sense of humour! I love you!

A huge thanks to Tiffany Skirrow, my incredible aligned soul bestie. My journey started with you and has grown into an amazing friendship along the way. I truly appreciate all your light, strength, love and your gentle heart.

And finally, thank you to the constant rock in my life, Brenda Kaye for everything you do!

Forewords

From the first time I heard Denise speak, I felt an instant connection. Her voice was so calming, yet confident. She had an incredible knowledge of all that she spoke about. I was mesmerized and could feel the joy that she brought to her entire audience each time.

At the time, I was still successfully teaching others how to manifest their lives on purpose but I was also was on an up-leveling path of my own spiritual journey, connecting with more of my spiritual gifts. I felt at comfort and ease, as if Denise knew exactly what I needed to hear at just the right time. Ahh, I was feeling that alignment we speak and hear so much about! Denise became one of my very close friends and I feel blessed each and every day to have her in my life.

This book, *The Key,* is the perfect timing where ever you are on your journey in this life. So many humans are living in reaction mode to what is going on around them and what others are saying and doing. *The Key* aligns with where you are right now at this very moment so you live your life from the inside out. You will begin to see changes within and around you. You will have inspired thoughts followed by inspired actions throughout this book. Money, abundance, your psychic gifts, guides, numbers, crystals, self-development, passion and these beautiful universal energies will all begin to align to where you are right now and further your beautiful journey.

I use all of these aspects in my everyday life and I feel free and abundantly full of joy and all that comes along with it. This book surely does have 'The Key' to unlock the brilliant magic that is already inside of you. Now, it's your turn.

Cathlene Miner, International Speaker, Author, Host, and Non-Profit Founder and President of Hopefull Handbags, Inc Global

Denise is one of the most beautiful lights I have the pleasure of calling a soul friend.

Meeting and being a part of Denise's journey has been a gift from the universe in itself - to be invited to write a foreword is an absolute honour.

I met Denise seven years ago and was immediately captivated by her mystical presence, her gentle energy and her ability to pour nurture and love over those that crossed her path. As I began to build a friendship with Denise it became obvious as to why my soul had completely fallen in love with hers. It wasn't until I found out that she too was a psychic that I understood why we bonded as quickly as we did.

Throughout our friendship together I have witnessed Denise grow her community as she has helped women across the globe to awaken their own universal magic through angelic activation, money mastery, numerology and many other metaphysical methodologies – supporting each woman to master their own spiritual brilliance and rising.

'The Key' is nothing short of otherworldly activation and magic upon each page – my wish is that this book lands within the hands of as many souls around the world as each of them are guided back home through Denise's teachings and the magic that's channelled through her.

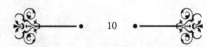

The world is ready for the next wave of awakened magic, and I know within the depths of my soul that this book and Denise's message will absolutely be a part of the process.

Tiffany Skirrow, Founder of When She Rises

Denise is an incredible light in this world. She makes spirituality something that the everyday person can understand. She's everybody's cheerleader and I know this book will enhance the lives of so many.

Leona Burton, CEO of MIB international, Author and Influencer

We have known Denise for two years through the online coaching world and we have absolutely adored watching her magical business journey. We have always felt drawn and aligned to collaborating with Denise as she has a kind and loving nature but also this magnetic undercurrent of empowering strength which inspires spiritual beings globally. Her honesty and ability to hold herself and everyone she meets in the most beautiful golden light, whilst genuinely celebrating success is extremely special and unique: a true gift. Denise is on one very special mission to enlightenment for herself and for everyone who is blessed with her presence. We are proud to know her and to continue to witness her wondrous journey unfolding.

Love, faith and a sprinkle of magic, LOA Twins
Tesha and Candice Matthew

Denise Martinez Rossini is the epitome of an earth angel who helps women across the globe to explore and embrace their own spiritual gifts. I connected with Denise almost two years ago at a time when I was ready to open up to my own spiritual gifts and she has been a pivotal part of my journey ever since. She is 'The Key' to thousands of women's spiritual journeys.

An expert in numerology, angels, crystals and lots more, Denise is so insightful and is continually learning and building on her knowledge. The more she learns, the more she shares. Lovingly guiding you to own your queen energy with her gentle, kind, caring and magical approach, Denise aids you to open your eyes to everything that is possible for you and helps you. Ultimately helping recognise that you deserve a life of love, joy and abundance. That is your birthright.

Sit back, relax and enjoy reading 'The Key', an engaging and compelling book which sets you on the path to your spiritual journey.

Divine love and light,
Marianne Jones, Intuitive Coach and Crystalologist at The Blossoming Collective

Introduction

*If you want to see universal magic,
you have to believe in it first!*

Who Am I?

My name is Denise Martínez Rossini. I'm an intuitive numerologist and Spiritual Empowerment Mentor. But for a long time, I didn't know who I was or where I fitted in. For as long as I can remember I felt like a square peg trying to fit in a round hole.

My home life though was wonderful. With loving parents and two younger brothers we had a very happy home, but I was always the wild child!

One of my favourite things as a young child was to listen to my 'nana' and the stories of our family she'd tell. It was during this time at around the age of 7 I became aware of my nana's gifts. She was a flame reader, tasseographer and was clairvoyant and claircognizant.

I used to love her teaching me to look into the flames to discover what I could 'see'. It was also around this time that I started to become aware of my own gifts and spiritual connections that would grow as I did.

My family weren't regular churchgoers but I found a faith within me that would also grow and be a constant rock for

me. I've attended various churches and also left various churches because I didn't feel aligned with some of their judgemental views.

One church, in particular, shocked me with extreme views which they accepted as normal. This started to form my views that you don't need to go to church to have faith. You can carry that within you and find it anywhere and at any time.

As I reached my late teens the awareness of my own gifts grew stronger, I'd often find myself being urged to pass on messages or knowing instantly a person's energy on meeting them.

Although I came from a gifted line whenever I mentioned my gifts or beliefs in a connection with angels or spirit it was met with 'don't let on to people you know that or they'll think you're crazy!' I started to be referred to as 'away with the fairies!'

As many women do I started to try and suppress my gifts from my late teens and early twenties. But when you have Clair gifts and energies they will keep pushing you until you let them out. So out they came but I never did anything with them I just accepted I had them.

I married in my late twenties and we had two beautiful children. Unfortunately, my marriage didn't last very long but I am still very fond of my ex-husband and we have remained close and are good friends. As a single mum whilst my children grew up times were quite tough. But I won't be telling you any sob stories here as they were also the happiest and love-filled times.

I decided to be a stay at home mum until my children were in full-time education at around the age of 4 and 5. I studied a lot during that time many subjects. Eventually, once the children were in school I opened my first business, a Holistic Therapy Clinic. I studied further and relished my

first encounter with Reiki, Crystals and Aromatherapy. It was during this time that my gifts led me to new understandings of Universal energies and the magic they can bring with them. My path then suddenly changed when I fell poorly and had to sell my clinic.

After taking some time out to recover, I continued on the next stepping stone of my journey. This took me to a quirky vibed place called Hebden Bridge in West Yorkshire. There I opened my Shabby Chic furniture shop and later a chocolate shop. It was whilst in my chocolate shop that my interest in numbers grew and I met my first Numerology mentor. I loved my times in Hebden Bridge and can honestly say it's the first time I felt I 'fitted in' anywhere! Gifts and spiritual vibes were completely open and accepted there and so my gifts truly came out and started to really shine!

It was also when my connection to Angels started and I realised I was channelling guidance. This then led me to come out of the spiritual closet and I found myself on my current path of becoming a Numerologist and Spiritual Empowerment Mentor. Little did I know at the start of this amazing part of my journey how incredible it would become!

I adore working with universal and angelic energies. My gifts and skills have excelled since becoming truly 'aware' of myself through Numerology and what I am here to do on my life journey. My path is to teach, inspire, motivate and empower. And to help as many women as I can to let their own gifts grow. To help them shine so their light can be shared with others too.

I have grown an amazing worldwide community of women who I help with both spiritual and business growth. I can see the light and energy within them and encourage them to let it uplift them with love and confidence.

My knowledge is expansive and also guided and I know I have *The Key* to helping others unlock the secrets of the

universe. This, in turn, will help them realise their own true life potential It was with this as the driving force which led me to write this book. I want to reach more women across the world to truly empower themselves from spirituality to abundance.

I have helped numerous women create and launch successful businesses around the world and have made some amazing friendships from my clients too. I have a VIP ACADEMY where members can delve deeper into their spiritual and business growth. I speak at many conventions and events for women on their journeys of empowerment.

The love and gratitude I feel for what I am blessed to do every day on my journey is immense. We were all born to live in love joy and abundance and I want to help as many as I can do just that! This is what led me to write this book. It's not a book in the usual sense. It's more of a guide to help you if you're going through an awakening or simply give you *The Key* to some of the most wonderful energies and connections.

ENJOY!

The Universal Nudge

Allow yourself to be guided by love

♥ Are you recently feeling different, excited but nervous at the same time?

♥ Are you experiencing a new sense of wanting to be seen and heard?

♥ Are you having an inner understanding that it's your time to shine!

♥ You know you're ready but not sure where to start.

♥ You may have heard the phrase 'spiritual awakening' being spoken about in different communities a lot lately, but it is still something a lot of women are unsure about or what it means.

WE ALL HOLD THE MAGIC!

If you're new to universal magic this is a great first step on your journey to success!

What is a spiritual awakening anyway? It can come to people in different ways. The first sign people tend to see is 11.11. Seeing this sign is like a massive nudge from the universe to tell you to wake up! When you see 11.11 acknowledge it, send up massive gratitude for having received it and ask

for guidance and more signs. You may find white feathers as signs around this time too. You may start to feel more in tune with your intuition and 'aware' of life itself. You may feel more 'awake' and notice nature more. The colours of the sky, grass and trees may seem brighter than before. The birds singing, the sea crashing against the waves and other naturally occurring sounds may be clearer to you than ever before.

You may have a new and great sense of excitement or have an energy that makes you want to jump for joy. You may have trouble sleeping especially between the hours of 3 am and 4 am. This is when many universally aligned souls have 'downloads' of new inspiration and ideas. You may be eager to seek both spiritual and universal knowledge and to venture into a whole new world!

2018
A YEAR OF
Enlightenment

2018 was a Universal Vibration of 11 in numerological terms. This meant the energy that year was one of illumination and inspiration. A year when many people started to feel the pull of the universe awakening them.

The previous 11th year of enlightenment before 2018 was 2009, a year where many felt a great change in their lives. It was a year when many went through endings and completions in their lives with big shifts being made. The last years that had an 11-year vibration were 1901 and 1910. This shows how

rare and special a year of enlightenment truly is. The sighting of 11.11 increased from around last October 2017 it led into the beautifully powerful year of 2018. People began to see it constantly throughout the day and many people still do now. It's important to point out at this point though, that you don't necessarily need to see 11.11 to realise you are going through a spiritual awakening. You can sense you are going through it from your intuition.

It is nothing to be afraid of at all. It is to be embraced and acknowledged as a wonderful stepping stone on your journey to success and enlightenment. There are ways you can work with it to become even more aligned with your own spiritual journey.

THOSE WHO BELIEVE ARE THE TRULY SIGHTED ONES.

11.11 JOURNALING TASK

If you have seen 11.11 when did it start happening for you?

_____

_____

_____

_____

_____

_____

Were there any life changes for you in 2009 and 2018?

_____

_____

_____

_____

_____

_____

_____

_____

_____

_____

_____

_____

_____

_____

_____

Universal Attraction

*Allow the Universe to shower
you with her kisses*

WHAT IS UNIVERSAL ATTRACTION YOU MAY BE WONDERING?

You're universally attractive when you are truly aligned with the universe and your own personal highest vibration. This can be achieved by embracing your own energy and working with universal magic. A positive mindset, following your inspired ideas with inspired action, is also important.

Living without doubting your own inner light and letting go of any negative limiting self-beliefs is key to this. It will become easier as you continue your journey and realise that other people's opinions of you don't matter as we are all on our own individual journey.

You should not let other people words hold you back. Emotion is a gift. It is a gift we can either choose to accept or to give it back to the gift provider.

For instance, if someone is trying to give you a negative emotion you can choose to ignore it by just witnessing it but not taking it on emotionally into your heart thereby leaving it with them. It is entirely your personal choice what you accept. Once you realise this it is so freeing.

One of the best ways to become universally attractive is working with the Law of Attraction with manifesting. It will become easier and more powerful if you connect with your crystals and angels and work with them alongside the universal vibration of the day and your personal chart. I will be covering all these subjects as we move forward within *The Key*. You don't need to become an expert in all of these subjects. You simply need to be open to work with them and follow the guidance you may receive either intuitionally or from your angels. For now, enjoy learning about all the different gifts and universal tools that are available to you.

YOU

Are you one of the many women who are awaking to their spiritual journey?

YOU FEEL IT IN YOUR BONES

You can't explain it because it's a feeling you've had for years but you know you are here to tread a special path even before it starts to fall into place. This is normal. Follow your intuition and it will guide you to the right stepping stones on your journey.

YOU CAN'T SETTLE FOR THE NORM

And you'll sometimes wish you could, believe me! Those who know they are here to be lightworkers, healers, mystics never follow a traditional path. Something in you will not allow you to settle for that even if there is part of you that wants to.

OTHERS DON'T GET YOU

There are going to be people who won't understand why you are drawn to 'the woo!' And at some point, you may have to let some of those people go so you can follow your true

path. Those that truly love you will encourage you without judgement or sometimes even understanding.

YOU'LL ATTRACT SYNCHRONICITIES

New people, new mentors, situations and experiences that appear in front of you just when you need them too. These are not coincidences they are guidance. Keep believing, keep going, and keep shining for you are *The Key* to someone else's path.

A SPECIAL PATH
JOURNALING TASK

What from the previous page resonates with you?

_____

_____

_____

_____

_____

_____

_____

_____

_____

_____

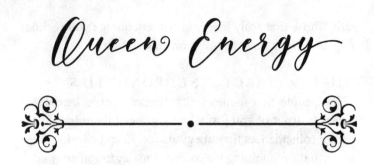

Queen Energy

You're a queen, call in your universal gifts

Queen energy is the true understanding that you are divinely loved. It is the knowledge that you absolutely deserve a life of love, joy and abundance.

Know that you deserve the best life and be fully open to receiving it. Know that you are strong and confident enough to embrace success with every breath you take.

Cleopatra, Nefertiti and Boudicca never doubted their queen energy or their right to claim their crowns. They stepped up into success without hesitation because those women knew who they were and what they could achieve. They OWNED their queen energy.

Once you fully claim your crown you will know that whatever you do, whatever you share, you do it because you are a queen! Your queen energy will help you grow, enjoy new adventures and achieve your dreams. You were born to shine, to make a difference on your journey and to empower others on their own journey too.

Being in alignment with your queen energy doesn't mean you need to be a queen who looks down on others or be disrespectful. We were all born equal and are connected through light. It means you should let yourself set an example of how we can all align ourselves with our queen energy.

BE A QUEEN. EMBRACE YOUR POWER AND LEAD WITH LOVE

Being a queen means having the inner knowledge that everyone has their own energy, no better or worse than your own.

WE'RE ALL GIFTED IN OUR OWN ENERGY

Some of us are psychics.
Some of us are artists.
Some of us are healers.
Some of us are teachers.
Some of us are creators.
Some of us are nurturers.
The list goes on and on…
A true queen knows she is not here to compete.
A true queen knows she is here to share her gifts.
A true queen knows she is here to support, empower and lead.

BE YOUR TRUE SELF! YOUR UNIQUENESS IS YOUR GREATEST GIFT

It's so important to be true to yourself above all else. If you are not true to yourself how can you be true to others? Knowing yourself is something that we can lose at times through the opinions of others and opinions that society puts upon us. People look towards someone who is true to their word and speaks authentically about themselves, their beliefs and values. People look for that now more than ever.
♥ Be authentic within your personal life.
♥ Be authentic within your business or career.
♥ Be authentic within your beliefs.

♥ Be authentic within your values.
Let your intuition guide you. If something doesn't feel right or has 'icky' energy then it's usually not right. Listen to your inner self. *Be true to yourself.*

QUEEN ENERGY
JOURNALING TASKS

Which queen energies do you see in yourself?

_____

_____

_____

_____

_____

_____

_____

_____

_____

_____

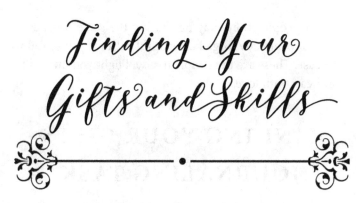

Finding Your Gifts and Skills

*The Universe is magical if you pick up
her tools and use them*

We are all blessed with skills and gifts in life. We also have abundant opportunities to grow and expand our gifts and skills. There are different ways to explore your gifts.

SELF-DEVELOPMENT

Some gifts are found through learning and development.

MENTORSHIP

A mentor is often a person who can see those gifts within you and help to bring them out. I believe we should all look for mentors throughout our life.

GROWTH

With our natural gifts of healing or a psychic gift allowing ourselves to grow with them and let them shine is so important. If you are naturally gifted don't hold back. Allow yourself to grow and shine.

CIRCLES OF LIGHT

The circle that you should align yourself with is that of like-

minded people. They may be sharing the same journey as you or have already forged a beautiful path for you to follow with ease. These are the people that will light you up and fill your heart with love.

FINDING YOUR GIFTS
JOURNALING TASK

List ways of how you can enhance any gifts you have

_____

_____

_____

_____

_____

_____

_____

_____

_____

_____

Grounding and Protection

Just Breathe!

Grounding yourself is an essential tool to help keep you on the right path and for keeping your energy and vibe aligned. The universe has given us some amazing tools to help us both stay grounded and in aligning our energy and vibration.

CRYSTALS

Crystals have amazing energies and help us to stay grounded especially when working with our clients.

NATURE

This is a truly wonderful way to ground yourself and blow away the cobwebs of negative energy too. Lift your chin up and let the sunshine down on your and the breeze blow away your concerns.

MEDITATION

Create or find yourself a beautiful guided meditation that you can connect with when you need to ground yourself.

PROTECTING YOUR ENERGY
It is your absolute birthright to be able to protect your energy and its beautiful light.

CRYSTALS – NATURE'S TREASURE!
There are many crystals you can use for energy protection such as: Amethyst, Smokey Quartz, Black Tourmaline, Selenite, Aventurine and Labradorite to name a few.

SAYING NO
You can be assertive without entering into an angry or agitated emotional state. Learn to politely refuse when you feel the need. Know your boundaries and put them in place.

NINJA WHINGERS
Be mindful of the people around you and who you allow to influence your energy. Are you surrounded by ninja whingers or low energy friends that want to sit on their pity potty daily?

Who you choose to have in your closest circle plays a major part in how it affects your energy. If you can, choose high vibe and positive minded friends and colleagues. If you know you you're unavoidably going to be around someone negative then take steps to prepare yourself for before meeting them.

ENERGY BUBBLES
Imagine a bubble of energy enclosing your body. You can either see the whole bubble forming around you wholly, or you can see it building slowly from the ground up and slowly surrounding you. Make sure it covers you from head to foot to keep out any negative vibes.

You can choose any colour for your bubble. Here are some examples of colour and the intention you can set with your bubble.

Clear for protection.
Purple for healing.
Pink for love.
Gold for abundance.
White for peace. You can keep refreshing the energy of your bubble as you wish.

GROUNDING & PROTECTION JOURNALING TASK

Look at your grounding and protection needs. How can you improve them?

_____

_____

_____

_____

_____

_____

_____

_____

_____

_____

Living Your Dream Life

A chance for you to truly soar!

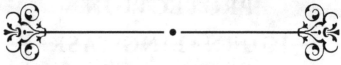

Live your life to the full.
It's not a rehearsal.

The best way to attract the life you truly want is to feel the energy of who you truly desire to be. Don't push how you want to live your dream life into the future. How often do we do that? We say when or if I get this or do that. And we always push it away from us as if it only lies just out of reach.

Even if you haven't accomplished what you truly desire yet you should be embracing the energy of it. This is where you can truly let your imagination run riot and in your mind's eye see yourself living your dream life. Don't hold back with what you ask for, it doesn't matter where you are on your journey; it's the destination that counts.

There are different ways to do this and you should do whatever feels best for you.

You can either write about your dream life self each day as if you are living it at this moment. Or you can spend 10 minutes each day visualising it. If you prefer, create a dream day vision board with how you would spend a typical day.

However you do this know that it really helps you to achieve what you truly want. Answer the following questions to help you build a clear picture of your dream life.

YOUR DREAM LIFE
JOURNALING TASKS

What is your ideal career?

_____

_____

_____

_____

_____

What is your ideal income?

_____

_____

What amount is your idea of happy money?

_____

_____

_____

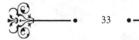

Where in the world would you like to live?

_____

_____

_____

What does your dream home look like?

_____

_____

_____

_____

_____

_____

What car would you love to drive?

_____

_____

What gift would you love to give back?

_____

_____

_____

_____

_____

What do you want to be known for?

_____

_____

_____

How do you want to inspire others?

_____

_____

_____

What does success look like to you?

_____

_____

_____

_____

_____

How you would spend a day in your dream life?

_____

_____

_____

_____

_____

_____

_____

_____

_____

_____

_____

_____

_____

_____

_____

_____

_____

Daydreaming

Inspiration starts from within.

STOP DAYDREAMING!

How many times did you hear that as a child? There you were imagining all sorts of amazing things and fantastic adventures when suddenly you hear 'sit up straight and stop daydreaming!' You felt your heart flop with a thump. Do you remember how heavy that made you feel? That was your vibe dropping like a stone.

Who knew how damaging those two words could be? You were being told to stop letting your mind create, stop letting your imagination grow and your self-worth soar.

Let me tell you something…

START DAYDREAMING!

By daydreaming your letting creative thought flow and feeding your subconscious mind with endless possibilities that you can achieve.

Daydreaming lets ideas turn into inspiration which eventually turn into light bulb moments for new ventures in life and business.

Don't just daydream, get journaling them. Treat yourself to a gorgeous journal - you know how much we all love pretty stationery!

Get your daydreams down and see the magic that'll come

from them and follow your flow. Take inspired action and watch possibilities grow into realities!

DAYDREAMING JOURNALING TASKS

Allow yourself to daydream throughout your day regularly. Create a list of inspired ideas you have whilst daydreaming that you can take inspired action on.

_____

_____

_____

_____

_____

_____

_____

_____

_____

_____

_____

_____

_____

Crystals

Embrace your own light.

Crystals have been used for healing purposes for thousands of years. They work with universal energy.

Everything in our world has its own vibrational energy. Crystals are one of the most stable forms of matter in the universe due to their formation. I love how Mother Earth gives us clues on how to use them by their colour formation too.

Grounding stones are mostly earthen colours such as black, browns and greys. While angelic connection crystals are mostly whites and pale blues. Healing crystals are mainly purples and greens. Abundance crystals are mainly golds and yellows. Intuitional crystals are mainly iridescent. Crystals for love and self-love show in various shades of pinks.

Isn't nature magical? Here are some of my favourites and how they can help you.

Crystal Energy

CLEAR QUARTZ

Clear Quartz is known as *The Master Crystal*. It brings clarity, awareness and peace of mind. It also promotes relaxation, healing and helps you keep balanced as a whole.

Interestingly this crystal is viewed by some (including myself) as male energy whereas its equivalent female energy crystal is Snow Quartz which has a beautiful gentle clarity with it.

There is a beautiful tale associated with Clear Quartz that when angels cry their tears fall to the earth and form into this wonderful crystal.

ROSE QUARTZ

Rose Quartz is your go-to crystal for love. It is especially useful for self-love, self-confidence and self-discipline. It opens your heart chakra and promotes inner peace.

Lots of the ladies in my social media community keep some Rose Quartz in their bra to help open their heart chakra!

CITRINE

Citrine is also known as *The Merchants Stone*. Citrine is a stone of abundance and brings joy and happiness too. It promotes prosperity and positive outcomes and can also help increase your creativity and imagination. A must-have crystal for manifesting!

AMETHYST

Amethyst helps to protect against negative energy. It helps with courage, inner strength and is a healing crystal. It is also useful for aiding peaceful sleep so pop a chunk under your pillow for a restful night.

LABRADORITE

Labradorite is also known as the *Magician's Stone*! It enhances psychic ability and awakens your inner spirit. Also a go-to crystal for growing your intuition and used as a protector from negative energy and misfortune.

PYRITE

Pyrite is also known as *Fools Gold*. This is a good stone to use for changing your money mindset from one of poverty to wealth. If you're an over-spender look for pyrite on Hematite to help ground your money energy.

LAPIS LAZULI

Lapis Lazuli is also known as the *Royal* or *Queen's stone*. This is because of its association with Cleopatra who is rumoured to have used it in her milk bathing ceremonies. It promotes truth and wisdom, helps with insight, intuition and self-awareness.

CARNELIAN

Carnelian promotes courage and confidence. It is useful for enhancing creative energy and communication skills and a stone that will help you speak authentically.

SELENITE

Selenite is a crystal that cleanses other crystals near to it and can cleanse the aura of negative energy. I always keep a big piece at my front door to cleanse people's energy on entering my house.

You can also use it for house cleansing if you struggle with the smell of sage. It is one of my favourite crystals for connecting with my angels too.

HEMATITE

Hematite is useful for meditating for mental clarity and grounding. It helps with organisation and memory and is a true crystal for strength and grounding.

TIGERS EYE

Tigers Eye empowers integrity and confidence. It promotes

personal power, confidence. and also helps release fear and anger.

PICTURE JASPER

Picture Jasper helps increase creativity and confidence. It helps us to break old habits as well as eases stress and anxiety. Look for your own story in the stones pattern picture.

AMETRINE

Ametrine is a really exciting stone which combines the qualities of Citrine and Amethyst. It helps with the manifestation of visions and promotes bringing your dreams into reality. It's a great stone to have with you when chasing late payment from clients.

SUNSTONE

Sunstone increases happiness, optimism and joy. Promoting happiness and it is uplifting. It really is a crystal full of sunshine!

MOONSTONE

Moonstone is a gorgeous milky creamy stone. It will help you open up with intuition, release stagnant energy and pulls in the feminine energy of the moon.

APOPHYLLITE

Apophyllite for me this is one of the most Angelic stones of all. Its angelic connection energy is just beautiful. It will often have inclusions of stilbite which has its own healing properties too.

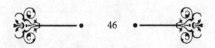

PLACING YOUR CRYSTALS

♥ Put them in your spiritual space if you have one.

♥ Keep them in your bedroom whilst you sleep or under your pillow.

♥ Wear them as a necklace or bracelet.

♥ Keep them in your pocket or purse.

♥ Meditate with them, setting your intentions of how you would like them to help you. Do not just plonk them all in a bowl together and forget about them!

I think it's best to keep them in their own properties collection too. For instance, I wouldn't put my grounding stones with angelic stones.

CRYSTAL DANCING

Keep your crystals moving to freshen their energy too. Move them around; give them a little dance to keep their energy bright!

CLEANSE AND CHARGE YOUR CRYSTALS

SAGE

Cleansing with sage has been a tradition for centuries. It is also a great way to cleanse your personal energy, as well as your spiritual space, and crystals too.

MOONLIGHT BATHING

Bathing your crystals in moonlight helps cleans and

recharges your crystal's energy. Place your crystals on a window or place them outside overnight. A full or new moon will give your crystals their greatest energy.

SELENITE

Place selenite near to your crystals or placing them on the selenite to cleanse them. Selenite can remove energy blocks from crystals as it has a natural ability to repel negative energy.

WATER

Holding your crystals under clear clean water is one of the simplest ways of cleansing your crystals. But make sure they are suitable for this method. For example, putting selenite into water would damage it.

Usually tumbled stones are fine with water as long as they not flaky like selenite, kyanite and other similar stones.

SETTING YOUR INTENTIONS WITH YOUR CRYSTALS

Hold the crystal in your non-dominant hand and begin to clear your mind of any thoughts. When setting your intention it's important to set it with gratitude in your heart.

Set your intention clearly, for example, don't just say 'send me money!' Instead, you could say, 'I am opening my heart with love and gratitude to receiving abundance.'

Fully connect with your crystal so it can feel your energy. It is thought that your left hand is for receiving energy and your right hand for giving.

MEDITATING WITH CRYSTALS

Embracing the energy of crystals is a wonderful way to meditate. It's a great way to connect to your angels, spirit

and universal energy too. Meditation can help to raise your awareness, heighten your intuition and bring new thoughts, ideas, or inspirations through. While meditating with crystals, you can wear them on you, hold in your hand, or place on your body.

Put on some relaxing music that helps your mind calm down, focus on your breathing, and begin to calm your mind.

These are some of the many different ways you can embrace the energy of your crystals. I hope you grow to love them as much as I do.

CRYSTAL JOURNALING
TASKS

List your favourite crystals

_____

_____

_____

_____

_____

_____

_____

_____

_____

_____

List any angelic, spirit or universal connections you've made working with your crystals

_____

_____

_____

_____

_____

_____

_____

_____

_____

_____

_____

_____

_____

_____

_____

_____

_____

Psychic Gifts

Spiritual knowledge is a gift.
Sharing it brings more gifts.

Have you ever wondered if you have a psychic gift, but you doubt yourself or think you are going crazy? Well, guess what, you're not the only one!

Most people I know who have psychic gifts have doubted their abilities at one time or another. Here's a little insight looking into our spiritual and psychic gifts and how to develop them.

Even if you don't want to develop your psychic gifts yourself but are curious about them I'm sure you will enjoy this chapter and find it interesting.But before that, the most important thing is to understand and honour a code of conduct for using psychic gifts and healings.

CODE OF CONDUCT

♥ You only do work for the good of others and yourself.

♥ Learn to ground yourself, open up and close off when doing readings.

♥ Understand it is your absolute right to protect your own energy.

♥ You are responsible for your own choices.

♥ You are always respectful and never get emotionally involved with those you are trying to help.

♥ Never use your gifts or healings without the consent of

the person you want to help.

♥ Client confidentiality is of the utmost importance and should never be disrespected.

The intuitive mind is a sacred gift and the rational mind is a faithful servant. We have created a society that honours the servant and has forgotten the gift. – Albert Einstein

CLAIRVOYANCE (CLEAR SEEING)

Clairvoyance is the ability to see visions of the past, present and future. These can be received via signs, dreams, visions, or picked up from people when reading. Clairvoyants may also have the ability to connect with spirit.

CLAIRCOGNIZANCE (CLEAR KNOWING)

This is when you just suddenly know something to be true, without even having seen it, heard it or felt it. It's just a soul knowing.

CLAIRAUDIENCE (CLEAR HEARING)

This is when you are able to hear a voice, sound and sometimes music from other realms. When connected with spirit these can be messages for someone.

CLAIREMPATHY (EMOTIONAL FEELING)

This is when you sense other people's emotions, thoughts and feelings. You can literally soak up their energy. It's important for empaths to protect their own energy so they don't become drained.

CLAIRSENTIENCE (PHYSICAL FEELING)

This is when you have a 'gut feeling' or when 'something just doesn't feel right,' and you feel it as a physical sensation, in your body.

CLAIRTANGENCY (CLEAR TOUCHING)

This is when you have the ability to have certain knowledge about an event or person by contact with them or something that belongs/belonged to them. This is also known as psychometry.

CLAIRALIENCE (CLEAR SMELLING)

This is when you have a connection through your sense of smell, such as a fragrance or aroma of a something, a person, place, or animal that is not connected in the reality of where you are. You may receive these smells spiritually rather than physically.

CLAIRGUSTANCE (CLEARTASTING)

This is when you receive insights through a sense of taste, without actually having that particular food or drink in your mouth. It could have been a favourite meal of someone connecting with you from spirit.

We all have the ability to develop gifts and usually find there are three that we have and can develop.

HONING YOUR SKILLS
AND GIFTS

JUST BEING

This can be practised by allowing yourself to be completely still and sensing what is going on around you.

Feel the weather on your face, stand and watch the light and shadows moving around you. Focus on every noise and movement going on around you feel them with every fibre of your energy.

Watch people going about their day. What they are wearing,

how they smell, what their energy feels like. You can almost go into a dream state whilst doing this; it feels like you are viewing things from afar.

LISTEN

Don't just listen with your ears. Listen with your mind and your emotions too. When someone is speaking to you fully feel their words from a place of love. Allow what they are saying to flow with your thoughts.

Remember though, emotion is a gift. If someone is speaking with words that don't come from a place of love then simply listen with your ears and not with your heart!

MEDITATION AND DAYDREAMING

One of the best ways to develop your own intuition is to meditate. This can help you to open up and for your gifts to grow naturally. By daydreaming you can take yourself to new heights and places that allow you to flow with magical energy. We did this a lot as children but were wrongly told to 'stop daydreaming!'

INTUITION

Do you ever get a feeling that something isn't quite right? Someone may be encouraging you to do something quite innocently, but you know instinctively it's the wrong thing to do. Or you may be on a journey when you suddenly know you need to take a different direction. Allow that 'gut feeling' of your intuition to guide you and that gift will grow stronger!

JOURNALING

Freewriting is a great way to develop your gifts. Pick up a pen and simply allow yourself to be guided in what you write without thought. What you write may surprise you You can also use journaling to write down any dreams, messages and

insights that you may receive. This will help you gain clarity into how your gifts are developing. You can look back on them for any relevance that might have been revealed to you.

TEST YOURSELF

There are some simple ways you can learn to test your abilities. Simple things like this will help you develop your gifts such as trying to guess who is knocking at the door before answering.

If you are going to meet a friend try and guess what colour outfit she may be wearing. When listening to the radio try and guess which song will play next.

PRACTICE

The old saying 'the more you practice the better you'll get' is very true! Allow your gifts to grow but don't try and force them too!

REMEMBER

To always protect your energy and follow the code of conduct!

PSYCHIC GIFTS
JOURNALING TASKS

Which psychic gifts do you have?

_____

_____

_____

_____

_____

_____

_____

_____

How can you develop your psychic gifts more?

_____

_____

_____

_____

_____

_____

_____

_____

_____

_____

_____

_____

Spirit Guides

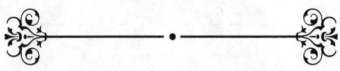

Be still and listen.

I thought I would share my knowledge of spirit guides with you as I think it's important to have a true understanding of them, especially if you're working as a medium. What's the difference between spirit guides and angels is a question I'm often asked. The way to answer this simply is this: angels are beings of light that have never lived in human form while spirit guides have lived as humans whether that is recently or from ages past.

Everyone has spirit guides; the number of spirit guides that we have can vary. Several spirit guides are common to everyone and some people have numerous spirit guides. However, here we are looking at the most well-known spirit guides.

MASTER SPIRIT GUIDE

This spirit guide is the main guide that looks over your life journey. Your master spirit guide is with you from birth and can help you with major changes with your lifetime. This guide can help you with direction and which way to turn.

PROTECTOR SPIRIT GUIDE

This spirit guide is like your own personal bodyguard. You can seek your protector spirit guide when you feel the nervous for your own safety physically, energetically or spiritually.

These spirit guides are often seen as warrior types. They are also sometimes seen in animal form such as wolves or lions.

HEALER SPIRIT GUIDE

This spirit guide is the 'medical officer' on your spirit team. Your doctor spirit guide oversees your emotional health and well-being. You can call upon your healer spirit guide to help you find the right remedies, herbs and essential oils or to help you feel more at ease.

TEACHER SPIRIT GUIDE

This spirit guide is a mentor and teacher for anything that you choose to learn in this lifetime. Learning is part of our overall life journey. Your teacher spirit guide helps you to find the right direction to topics and subjects and teachings that can help you grow in your own light.

JOY SPIRIT GUIDE

Your joy spirit guide is the guide that helps put a spring in your step. Joy spirit guides are often envisioned as mischevious, fun and free-spirited. They are the magical guides that can connect you with your inner child magic. They also show themselves through the magical realms as unicorns, fairies, elves and dragons. They can wake up the magic within us.

ANCESTORAL SPIRIT GUIDE

These are guides that may have been a relative recently or they can be from our ancestral past. They can bring wisdom, guidance and strength. They are sometimes seen as figures as they appeared throughout history.

GATEKEEPER SPIRIT

This spirit guide is the 'connector' of your spirit team, they

are an important guide if you are working as a psychic or medium.

Your gatekeeper spirit guide can help you receive a better connection between or clearer picture with other spirits. They can show you signs and pictures if you are having trouble getting trueness from a spirit you are connecting with during a reading.

You can connect with your spirit guides if you wish to do so within meditation by asking them firstly their name and then opening up a communication with them. Some people don't always connect with spirit guides especially if they have a strong connection with their angels. As with all spiritual connections and learnings it's a personal choice.

SPIRIT GUIDES
JOURNALING TASK

Have you connected with your spirit guide? Write how the connection happened.

_____

_____

_____

_____

_____

_____

_____

_____

_____

_____

_____

_____

_____

Which of the spirit guides have you connected with?

_____

_____

_____

_____

_____

_____

What did they share with you?

_____

_____

_____

_____

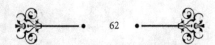

Angels

I am open to receiving love from my Angels.

For me, connecting with the Angels is one of life's true blessings. I love working with them and am always amazed at the guidance I receive from them. It forms a big part of my work and the knowledge I receive and share. Angels are recorded from the beginning of time and all corners of the world.

Angels are beings of light. They are here to guide us to live a life of light and love. It is up to us to be open to receiving their beautiful light and guidance.

Connecting with Angels

PRAYER

Prayer is the simplest way to connect with your angels. Speak with God, the universe, a higher power, whatever your belief or faith. It's always best to speak from a place of love and gratitude and not fear or lack.

Know that your words are listened to with love, the highest energy of all. Just speak openly and calmly and ask for guidance and help you'd like. You can speak out loud or silently from your heart.

MEDITATION

'Ask in prayer, listen in meditation' is a phrase many of us have come to know. But an answer to your prayers can come at any time or anywhere. Just sitting quietly and listening can help. But if you are more comfortable listening in meditation there are many simple ways to meditate.

The simplest way is to just sit and concentrate on your breathing whilst connecting. If you would like to connect with a certain angel imagine this angel with you.

If you know their light colour, crystals or aroma this can sometimes help too. Open up your heart to receiving love and guidance.

SPIRITUAL SPACE

Create a sacred space in the corner of your room, dressing table, desk or even a shelf if you have limited space. You can place crystals and objects that you find special there. This is the space where you may like to spend special time each day in reading, journaling or connecting with your angels.

Take a deep breath as you enter your spiritual space, and imagine being bathed in a beautiful life as you do.

GO OUT IN NATURE

Get out into your spiritual energy zone in nature. This can be the energy space that you're magically drawn too. A lot of women are drawn to the sea; some find they can connect with their spiritual vibe more on a beach, or in a forest. For others, it can be in a desert or mountain range. Wherever stirs your soul is your energy zone.

Allow the beauty of nature to fill up your senses, what can you see, hear and smell. Connect with nature through the power of touch and let the magic enter your body through your fingertips. This can light up your soul. Then when you feel ready ask your angels to step in and embrace a connection

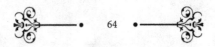

with you. If you would like to connect with a specific angel you can also ask them for a sign.

MUSIC

Music is a beautiful way to connect with your angels. One of my clients had a beautiful first experience with her angels this way.

It was a very special moment for her and one that I love to hear told. She has gone on to be an angel artist with the guidance she received whilst connecting. You can ask your angels to connect through a song that has a special meaning to you. Listening to binary music also has a beautiful resonance to help with connecting.

JOURNALING

Keeping a journal is a beautiful way to record your connection with angels. You can enter any signs, messages and feathers you receive. Your journaling doesn't have to be perfect word for word. It's not like being back at school!

You could start by simply writing down your thoughts and feelings about your connections or prayers. Journaling can grow into a beautiful experience in itself.

You can attach any feathers you find or other signs that you've received such as flower petals or coins.

Why not fill your journal with beautiful images as well as words. You can sketch any images you receive of or from your angels.

Don't worry if you don't see an angel in full image at first. This can be a connection that grows over time. You could also fill your journal with beautiful aromas to by anointing pages with a dab of your favourite essential oil. Why not embellish your journal with a few of your favourite crystals or angel charms too.

Choirs of Angels

THE FIRST SPHERE

THE SERAPHIM

The Seraphim are the highest angels. These angels look after heavenly movements and pass the divine light to the other angels and all living creatures of the world.

THE CHERUBIM

These angels are the scholars of the heavens. They have unlimited knowledge and divine wisdom. They inspire spiritual renewal.

THE THRONES

The Thrones are the peacemakers who bring harmony when there's negativity. They bring spiritual perfection and divinity to the universe. They help the connection between the veils of the visible and the invisible.

THE SECOND SPHERE

THE DOMINIONS

The dominions work mainly in the spirit realm. They don't often get involved with earthly concerns – they concentrate more on guidance for other angels. They are sometimes also known as 'flashing swords.'

THE VIRTUES

The virtues are the angels known to give us signs and create miracles. They like to give us a gentle little nudge of encouragement when we are struggling on our life journey.

THE POWERS

These angels are known as warrior angels. They ward off evil and defend the unprotected and help you with confidence and your own power.

THE THIRD SPHERE

THE PRINCIPALITIES

The prime responsibility of these angels is to look over our planet. They can help us when we are lost in a strange place. Have you ever been to a city and don't know which way to turn? Then find the one you take is the right way. No coincidence, its angelic guidance!

ARCHANGELS

The archangels are the 7 angels that help us within all areas of our lives. The archangel's purpose is to help us through the guidance of love and light. You can summon the archangels for help and guidance whenever you are in need.

ANGELS

These are best known as our guardian angels. Your guardian angel is with you from birth and will be with you all of your life. Your angels often work together too in helping to bring you the best guidance. Isn't it a beautiful comfort to know that you are so divinely loved by your angels?

THE 7 ARCHANGELS

The archangels are the angels I mostly connect and work with through my channelling. The archangels are different from your guardian angels that are with you constantly throughout your life.

I like to think your guardian angels help you with day to day practicalities such as finding a parking space, helping with lost items and energy protection. The archangels I believe help you with larger life guidance, such as your gifts, health, relationships, work and your overall life journey. You can call upon all your angels whenever you want. These are the 7 Archangels and their associations.

MONDAY ARCHANGEL GABRIEL

Archangel Gabriel will help you with guidance through messages, signs and connecting with your intuition.

TUESDAY ARCHANGEL CHAMUEL

Archangel Chamuel can help you with guidance to increase self-confidence and the strength in letting yourself be seen and heard.

WEDNESDAY ARCHANGEL RAPHAEL

Archangel Raphael can help you heal and guide you safely on your travels.

THURSDAY ARCHANGEL ZADKIEL

Archangel Zadkiel will help you with guidance to opportunities, abundance and to be benevolent.

FRIDAY ARCHANGEL URIEL

Archangel Uriel will help you with guidance receiving love in all its glorious forms. Uriel can help you accept self-love.

ARCHANGEL JOPHIEL

Archangel Jophiel brings a sense of joy to your work and tasks and helps you feel a sense of serenity when needed.

SUNDAY ARCHANGEL MICHAEL

Archangel Michael will give you the strength to shine your light and help protect you from negative energies. Archangel Michael works with many other angels to help guide and protect us with divine love.

ANGEL EXPERIENCES

Once you become comfortable in being open to connecting with your Angels you may find you experience one or more of the following!

ANGEL SPARKLES

This is the term I choose to use for the beautiful little dancing lights or sparkles you may start to catch out of the corner of your eye. They can often catch you unaware and disappear just as quickly as they first appear.

ANGEL STROKES

The first time I experienced these I thought I'd walked through a spider's web! These usually start with extremely tiny strand-like strokes on your arms or face. They can grow stronger as your connection grows too feathery like strokes.

You may also have a vision of beautiful big white angel wings and may hear the ruffle of them too or the breeze as they unfold.

COLOURED LIGHTS OR ORBS

These are usually slightly bigger and brighter than angel sparkles. They can often appear just as white orbs but more often than not are coloured. Angels are beings of light and

you can learn to realise which angel it is you're connecting with through their colours.

It's important to note people don't always see or have signs of angels in the same way. There is no point in getting distracted from or putting pressure on yourself when connecting. You will come to recognise your angels by the way they show themselves to you in colour, sign or image.

IMAGE

Not everyone will see a full angel stood before or near them. There is no need to feel afraid when connecting. You will never be overwhelmed with more than you can cope with. Having said that, there is nothing more beautiful once you are ready, than seeing your angels. They can show themselves as male or female, again you will come to recognise them as they show themselves to you. More often than not it's usually archangel Michael that people first connect with, then either archangel Gabriel or archangel Raphael. Whichever way you connect enjoy this beautiful experience and don't forget to journal it!

ANGELS JOURNALING TASK

Have you connected with your angels?

_____

_____

_____

_____

_____

_____

_____

_____

How did your connection happen and where were you?

_____

_____

_____

_____

_____

_____

_____

_____

_____

_____

_____

_____

_____

List any signs you have received from your angels.

_____

_____

_____

_____

_____

_____

_____

_____

_____

_____

_____

_____

_____

_____

_____

_____

_____

Numerology

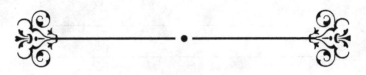

Gratitude is the key to abundance.
Open the door to opportunity.

Numerology is my favourite universal gift to work with. For me, numerology is the language of the universe. It gives incredible insight into whole areas of our life and understanding the vibrational energy of life itself.

SO WHAT IS NUMEROLOGY EXACTLY?

Numerology is said to have first been calculated by Pythagoras and other great philosophers such as St. Augustine of Hippo. Numerology is the ancient science of numbers and letters. Each number and letter has its own unique universal vibration relatable to the story of all of our lives.

Having a numerology reading will help you discover your personality strengths, how people perceive you and your true life potential. I truly believe everyone should have their chart read to empower themselves.

There are different systems across the world such as the Chaldean system. The system I use is the Western Pythagorean system. Your chart is made up of 7 core numbers each bringing their own understanding of you through their vibrational energy.

YOUR CORE NUMBERS ARE...

LIFE PATH NUMBER

Your life path number is the first of the two major numbers in your chart. This number shows who you truly are as a person. It's like your universal makeup.

DESTINY NUMBER

Your destiny number is the second most important number in your chart. Your destiny number shows the path you are meant to follow on your life journey. It also provides great guidance for career choices.

SOUL NUMBER

Your soul number reveals your heart's desire and how you may see yourself too. You can almost feel the tug on your heartstrings when you know and understand it!

PERSONALITY NUMBER

Your personality number is the 'outer you!' It is how you appear to people and how they perceive you in life. It shows you which of your particular life gifts shines through to others.

MATURITY NUMBER

Your maturity number comes into fruition from 40 to 50 years of age. This shows which gifts you have gathered on your journey or grown into.

BIRTHDATE NUMBER

Your birth date number is found in numerology by reducing down your birth date to a single digit. It's important

as it shows skills and gifts you will have naturally from birth that will help you achieve your true life purpose.

CURRENT NAME NUMBER

Your current name number is taken from the name you are using and currently known by. Your current name number enhances your energy with the gifts its vibration brings to you. Each of these numbers is calculated by their universal vibration to show the gifts skills and traits that make up your numerology chart.

Here's a simple explanation of how to calculate your own life path number.

Your LIFE PATH number is calculated by reducing down and adding across the numbers of your birth date.

*An important point to note here is how the birth date is written across different nations. e.g. in the UK, we write it as birth day, month, year.

In the US it is written birth month, day, year. It is very important you get the date flow correct as it will affect the birth date when calculating a full chart.

For this example, I will be using the UK system of date of birth: day, month, year.

So let's use Mary Lynn Jones
15th December 1968

Firstly you reduce the numbers down
15/12/1968

This becomes
1+5
1+2
1+ 9 + 6 + 8 = 24 = 2 + 4 = 6
636

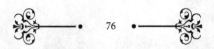

Then add across 6 + 3 + 6 =15 = 1+5 = 6

So the life path number for 15/12/1968 is 6.

You always reduce digits down to a single number except an 11, 22 or 33 as these are master numbers.

Master numbers have higher vibrational energy and can bring special gifts with them.

Here the different personalities of the numbers that make up a numerology chart. You may recognise yourself in these numbers. Having a full reading will truly reveal your gifts, skills and traits.

1. THE INDEPENDENT LEADER
Independent
Headstrong
Brave
Individual
Determined
Ambitious

2. THE PEACEFUL ONE
Patient
Supportive
Intuitive
Nurturing
Cooperative
Peaceful

3. THE CREATIVE EXPRESSIONIST
Creative
Optimistic
Friendly
Charismatic
Expressive
Imaginative

4. THE DEDICATED WORKER
Hardworking
Grounded
Reliable
Organised
Focused
Practical

5. THE FREE ONE
Fun
Adventurous
Adaptable
Pioneering
Enthusiastic
Imaginative

6. THE CARING ONE
Loving
Caring
Generous
Responsible
Supportive
Nurturing

7. THE SPIRITUAL ONE
Independent
Intuitive
Spiritual
Creative
Psychic
Philosophical
Inspirational

8. THE MANIFESTER
Energy Attractive
Self Motivated
Driven
Authoritative
Cultured
Entrepreneurial

9. THE COMPASSIONATE HUMANITARIAN
Generous
Compassionate
Broadminded
Sympathetic
Tolerant
Passionate
You may also have one of the three master numbers in your chart.

11. THE ENLIGHTENED ONE
Inspirational
Charismatic
Visionary
Illuminating
Spiritual
Optimistic

22. THE MASTER BUILDER
Organised
Visionary
Wise
Inspired
Planner
Dedicated

33. THE COSMIC PARENT

Dutiful
Kind
Generous
Loving
Nurturing
Devoted

You can use numerology for insight into so many different areas such as: Yyour own life chart reading.

Your child's reading.

Yearly forecasting.

Monthly and daily forecasting.

Business name analysis.

House energy readings.

Personal money energy readings.

Understanding universal messages.

I have read so many charts but I still find it fascinating to discover a person's gifts, skills and traits through their reading. It's amazing also, to see how numbers come down in family charts similar to names. Master numbers can be followed down through ancestry too.

I find it fascinating how children's charts have changed over the past decade or so too. We are seeing a lot more enlightened children from this time period.

I adore teaching numerology too. I love sharing the magic of the universe and seeing it light people up!

NUMEROLOGY
JOURNALING TASK

Calculate your own life path number and see if you recognise traits in yourself. Then why not try calculating friends and family members. My Life Path Number is...

_____

_____

_____

_____

_____

_____

_____

_____

_____

_____

_____

_____

_____

Recurring Numbers

May your heart be lifted by wings of love.

I receive so many messages about recurring numbers. Most people see them at some point during their life. You may know about angel numbers already but did you know recurring numbers carry two forms of messages?

The first is angel numbers which are divine messages. But there are also universal messages which are like little daily nudges of guidance through numerology. Here I explain the simple meaning of both.

ANGEL MESSAGES

Your angels communicate messages with you in the form of numbers They do this in various ways. Firstly you may start seeing 11.11.

Seeing 11.11 is your spiritual awakening call, a true blessing to show you are divinely loved and it gives you a great opportunity for manifesting with gratitude.

Always send up gratitude on seeing it and take note of your thoughts at the time. You can ask for angelic guidance to help you with all the numbers messages you receive.

111 – Monitor your thoughts carefully, and be sure to only think about what you want, not what you don't want. Focus your thoughts to the positive.

222 – You're planting seeds for success that will bring you rewards further on.

333 – You are surrounded by the highest divine love. Whenever you see patterns of 3 is a good time to connect with your angels and ask for guidance.

444 – This is a message for you not to worry. The angels are aware of your situation and want to reassure and guide you.

555 – Change is coming but you do not need to worry. It is just part of your natural life's flow. It could be something you have been praying for too.

666 – Your thoughts may be a little unbalanced at present. You are being guided to concentrate more on love and kindness than materialism. Do good deeds, show kindness and love for others.

777 – The angels are congratulating you on what you are doing. Keep focused on your journey and know you are heading in the right direction. You can achieve your dreams.

888 – It is a great time to reap the rewards of all your hard work. It's time to enjoy your success!

999 – You might be coming to the end of a certain phase of your life. This is also a message for you to consider taking on a concern such as the environment or an animal welfare cause.

000 – A gentle reminder you are at one and loved by your God. A situation might have come full circle for you too.

UNIVERSAL NUMEROLOGY MESSAGES

Sometimes the universe can send you messages that are meant to help you and give you guidance alongside your divine messages.

Even though seeing these repetitive numbers may drive you mad at times, it's better that you acknowledge them and know what they mean as they can be highly beneficial to you. These universal messages can give you a more direct day to day approach in helping you on your life journey.

So let's have a look at these numbers and what their significance could mean to you and how they can possibly help you with their meanings.

You may see numbers such as 222, 333 or 555. These are easily understood by looking at what each number means individually.

RECURRING 1s

Embrace your independence and individuality. It might be time for you to step forward from the crowd and tread new paths on your own journey. This is also a sign of new beginnings.

RECURRING 2s

Take some time to bring a sense of balance and harmony to yourself. You may want to spend some time in peace and quiet.

RECURRING 3s

You are being urged to express yourself more creatively. Don't take yourself too seriously. Remember it's important to have fun and let your hair down on occasion. Don't be afraid to let yourself be seen and heard!

RECURRING 4s

You need to stop and take some time to ground yourself. Take notice of your relationship with money, is it a healthy one? If you persist and persevere know that success can be yours and that you are being encouraged!

RECURRING 5s

You may need to make some changes so your energy can flow easily. Try thinking outside of the box and don't be afraid to take a leap of faith. This may be an opportune time for you to travel too.

RECURRING 6s

This is a message to let you know that love is on its way to you but may appear in any manner of ways! It's a time for you to treat yourself so you feel more in tune with your femininity. Spend some time with your loved ones whether that's with friends or family.

RECURRING 7s

Pay attention to your spiritual self. This may be a time for you to take up some personal and spiritual self-development.

RECURRING 8s

Monitor your thoughts at all times. Keep them positive. Balance the material and spiritual sides of your life. You are entering a period of what could be great abundance for you. Practice your manifesting skills.

RECURRING 9s

Something may be coming to an end. Let go of what doesn't serve you or is holding you back. There may also be the energy of healing around you, for you or for you to give to others.

RECURRING NUMBERS
JOURNALING TASK

List the recurring numbers you see and what their message may mean for you.

_____

_____

_____

_____

_____

_____

_____

_____

_____

_____

_____

_____

_____

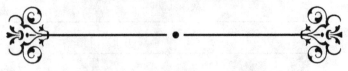

Karma

CREATE GOOD KARMA

Give as you would like to receive.

TELL THE TRUTH

The saying 'honesty is the best policy' is a good guide to use in life. What we give out reflects back to us. Therefore if we tell the truth we will receive the truth too.

It is always better to have truthful people in your life rather than untrustworthy people. Being authentic is something we should all adhere to.

LIVING YOUR TRUE LIFE PURPOSE

'Life is not a dress rehearsal' is one of my favourite quotes. Live your life to the full. Go after your dreams and help as many people as you can along the way.

The true key to success is helping others become successful. This is then reflected back to you. When you are aligned with your true life the universe will shine all its magical gifts upon you.

HELP PEOPLE

Helping others creates good karma because others will be more likely to help you in return should you need it. Helping others is one of life's true pleasures that will fill up your heart with joy.

MEDITATE

Pay attention to your thoughts and keep a positive mindset. Spending time in meditation or simply quiet time is good for your mind as well as your soul. Practice at least 10 minutes a day just 'being.'

PRACTICE COMPASSION AND KINDNESS

Life is a lot easier when it is in true flow. Giving and receiving in beautiful harmony together. Try and do little acts of kindness whenever you can. It's what makes the world go round!

KARMA JOURNALING TASK

How do you feel you can you align your energies so they are more balanced and in harmony with your karmic flow?

_____

_____

_____

_____

_____

_____

_____

_____

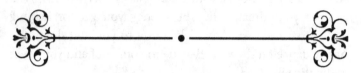

Money Magic

*Get your money story straight, not formed
by other people's words.*

Firstly let's talk about money. Why is it included in a book about spirituality and universal magic? I think a key to living abundantly and in alignment is to truly understand the energy of money. There are so many old money stories and beliefs that are untrue.

Money work is a big part of what I do in helping to empower women. So it had to be included. Let's look at some Money Magic, shall we?

CLEAN BRIGHT AND SHINY MONEY

This is money that lovingly flows with high vibrational energy. It will attract more clean money with a high vibration too. The cleanest money comes as a reward for doing good things honestly. This is the money you want.

DIRTY MONEY

This is money that has a vibration that's totally out of sync with the universe. As you can imagine the dirtiest money comes from crime – things like drugs, robberies or fraud. Maybe this is why getting rid of it is called laundering. This is the money you don't want.

Dirty money can be sneaky! If you're in business you get

an 'icky' feeling about the way you are receiving money through your business then give it a miss. For instance, don't sell a product you know to be of poor quality or faulty. You want to attract money with clean energy that will help you achieve your dream life. The money you get for helping a client succeed will flow deliciously to you and do a little happy dance on the way! Be true to your soul and your own authentic vibration.

SHINY VS DIRTY MONEY
JOURNALING TASK

List the ways in which you can bring in shiny money

_____

_____

_____

_____

_____

_____

_____

List the ways in which you can avoid dirty money

_____

_____

MONEY MONSTER STORIES

We have been told money monster myths from childhood. Let's look at them and see if you recognise how you've been misled with these stories.

'YOU SHOULD BE MORE CONCERNED WITH HELPING PEOPLE THAN MAKING MONEY!'

Believe me, you can help more people with money than you can without it. Being rich is a good thing. Don't carry childhood fairy-tale misconceptions that the rich are the baddies and the poor are the goodies. It's the type of person that you are that matters, not the amount of money you have or don't have.

I WOULD RATHER BE HAPPY THAN RICH!

If you want to be poor and happy, good for you! But that's just you. If you were rich you could be even happier by helping others that didn't want to be poor. Think about it. Happiness grows through sharing. Think of all the good you could do.

I MIGHT WIN THE LOTTERY ONE DAY!

Yes, you might, but why not get off your butt and make your own magic. Don't waste your time dreaming of slim chances. Put your dreams to good use with inspired action and build something for yourself that will bring all your desires into reality.

MONEY DOESN'T LIKE ME

Money doesn't care who you are, its energy. It doesn't have emotion. You need to look at your self-esteem. Build yourself up and give off the right energy to attract money.

THERE'S NOT ENOUGH MONEY TO GO ROUND!

There is more than enough money to go round. It's there for the asking. Do you think a successful business person thinks, 'oh I'd better stop working now because there's not enough money to go round!' No, of course, they don't!

I'M NOT CLEVER ENOUGH TO MAKE MONEY!

Absolute rubbish! You don't have to be a genius to be successful. If you have a spark of entrepreneurship and self-belief you can achieve great things in life. It all starts with you and your energy!

MONEY MONSTER STORIES JOURNALING TASK

List any old money monster stories you need to slay

_____

_____

_____

_____

_____

_____

_____

_____

_____

_____

_____

_____

_____

_____

TRUTH BOMB!

Sometimes you have to tell yourself it's time to get off your pity potty and take action. Stop listening to all the dumb chatter about money!

MONEY CHATTER

How do you perceive money? Do you say things like...

♥ Money isn't everything.
♥ I never have enough money.
♥ I'd love that, but I can't afford it.

Try and change your mindset around money. Say things like…

♥ Money is a wonderful energy.
♥ Money flows easily to me.
♥ I know I can afford that if I choose to save for it.

Be in control of your money. Treat it with respect.

Keep account of your spending and bills coming in. Pay what you can on time and then work out a plan to clear any outstanding debts. Be clear on your emotions. Don't hold negative ones. Be grateful for what money you do have.

MONEY CHATTER
JOURNALING TASK

What money chatter do you need to change?

_____

_____

_____

_____

_____

_____

_____

_____

_____

_____

_____

_____

_____

_____

_____

_____

YOUR MONEYSHIP

What is your relationship like with money? How is your moneyship? Imagine your money as your partner, let's look at what happens.

If your partner wants to go out and you moan, sulk and fret they won't come back every time they do, your partner will leave you for a more loving relationship. So will your money.

If you constantly moan to your family and friends about your partner not being there for you, your partner will leave you for a more harmonious relationship. So will your money.

If you are happy to see your partner go out because you love and trust them to return, your partner will be happy to come back as they love you and your relationship. So will your money.

If you tell your family and friends how much you love your partner and how wonderful your relationship is, your partner will love you even more and shower you with gifts large and small. Flowers, chocolates, shoes, a car even a home. So will your money!

MONEYSHIP JOURNALING TASK

How can you improve your moneyship?

_____

_____

_____

_____

GIVING INTENT TO MONEY

Decide what you want to spend your money on. Money is an energy that needs to flow. So give it a purpose.

Set your intention. Use a money mantra and put in the amount you want. 'I am so excited to be easily receiving... right now.' Feel a sense of excitement that it's coming whilst saying your mantra. You have to take inspired action for the money to come. Don't just sit and wait for it!

Think of ideas of how you can create energy for the money to flow in. Do you have a business idea you can start? Do you have a way to increase your existing clients? You can ask the universe to help you with this through prayer and meditation. Do whatever you can from your heart and to the best of your ability to help create the magic.

Remember money is energy and will be attracted to your highest vibration. Seal it all with gratitude, faith and trust that it will happen.

MONEY INTENTIONS JOURNALING TASK

What intentions are you going to set for yourself?

_____

_____

_____

_____

ABUNDANCE PASSWORDS

Let's take a look at your passwords. All your social media platforms, money transfer accounts, savings, bank account, email... you get the idea! They should all be abundant passwords to create universal attraction.

WORDS AND PHRASE IDEAS
- ♥ 20k in the bank
- ♥ Money in abundance
- ♥ Overflowing prosperity
- ♥ Millionaire mindset
- ♥ Rich
- ♥ Abundant
- ♥ Wealthy
- ♥ Gold
- ♥ Millionaire
- ♥ Successful

The numbers 1, 5, 7, and 8 are numbers of success and money energy. Use these numbers to attract abundance in passwords. Try not to use them in a recurring sequence for security but you can mix them up.

MONEY PASSWORDS
JOURNALING TASK

List your new abundance passwords

_____

_____

_____

_____

_____

_____

_____

YOUR PERSONAL MONEY SIGN

We all receive signs and messages from the universe. Being open to receiving and acting upon them is entirely up to us.

We can connect with our own money sign to show us we are heading in the right direction or when we should pay particular attention to something. Your personal money sign can be found in two ways.

1. YOU MAY HAVE ALREADY RECEIVED A SIGN

Think about a certain time when something amazing happened to you that was related to money. Did you notice anything related to this moment like seeing a certain flower, animal, letter or number? Have you seen it again since and wondered why? This is your money sign!

2. CHOOSING YOUR SIGN

Your money sign should not be related to any other signs you ask for. It should only be asked for in relation to money guidance.

Again you can choose a certain flower, animal or even a shape. You can ask for this sign whenever you would like guidance or use it when you are working on your money mindset, working with the law of attraction or setting your moon intentions.

Your energy and however you decide to charge it spreads for around 1.5 kilometres from you. That energy ripples through everything it comes into contact with. Imagine if all you ever sent out was positivity!

You could light up the world around you and imagine what that would do to your money energy flow. By shining, you are a magnet to all things abundant!.

MONEY SIGN JOURNALING TASK

What is your personal money sign?

_____

_____

_____

How did you receive it?

_____

_____

_____

_____

_____

_____

_____

_____

_____

_____

_____

_____

_____

_____

_____

_____

_____

_____

FANTASISE ABOUT YOUR MONEY!

How easy is it for you to fantasise about what you want in your life! Some people love to do this and soak it all up. Some people hate to do it and are afraid to imagine what they want.

A common thought is 'if I let myself want something too much, I will be devastated if I don't get it. So it's better not to think about it at all.' If this describes you, you need

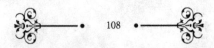

to challenge this fear and open up to the possibility to visualising what you truly want in life.

Without being able to imagine it, you are blocking achieving it. When you feel relaxed, open yourself up to letting your imagination flow and truly welcoming in your dream life. Would you love a trip to Paris? A fabulous huge diamond ring? A new car? Your dream house? Whatever it is, give yourself permission to want it, first of all with all your heart. This will pave the way for you to have it.

List your money fantasies and let your imagination run wild!

MONEY FANTASIES JOURNALING TASK

What money fantasies get you excited?

_____

_____

_____

_____

_____

_____

_____

_____

AUTHENTICITY

Being authentic is one of the biggest tips I can give when it comes to making money. Have integrity in all that you do. Having authenticity will truly make you stand out from the crowd. People will get to know your values, trust in you and want to work with or buy from you.

Skimping and cutting corners to save a few pennies doesn't work. Putting your name to something you don't believe in or have little knowledge of will see you fall. Be true to your word and you will succeed.

GIVE VALUE

What do you have that can solve someone's problem? This can be a gift, skill or product. If you have the solution people will come to you for it.

If you genuinely care in helping someone to find a solution to their problem they will tell people about you.

TAKE RISKS

Opportunity might knock on your door but it will only wait so long for you to answer. What if it doesn't work and you fail? So what! Get up and try again.

Every entrepreneur I know has tried and failed before succeeding. The risks of a saleable knowledge business are minimal. There are no massive overheads in selling knowledge and no stock to be purchased. For me, this is an absolute no brainer when it comes to spreading your wings and flying. It is one of the biggest growing industries in our online world now.

And it's women entrepreneurs that are creating amazing incomes from it. Just do it! What have you got to lose?

GIVE BACK

In order to keep receiving it is absolutely essential for you to keep giving! Are you offering something for free? This is a great way to first create interest in you and what you do. It doesn't have to be a huge gift. It can be a sample of your knowledge or product.

Once your money energy is flowing and growing you need to feed that energy with gratitude and generosity. Think of what you can contribute to or pay it forward for those who may need what you have to offer.

MONEY IS GOOD

Don't be ashamed of wanting to make money at all. It's how you make it that matters, not the amount you make. Make money through your skills gifts, knowledge or creativity, but most of all through authenticity.

MONEY AUTHENTICITY & VALUE JOURNALING TASK

List the ways in which you are authentic with your money energy

_____

_____

_____

_____

_____

_____

_____

_____

_____

_____

List how you give value to your money energy

_____

_____

_____

_____

_____

_____

_____

_____

_____

_____

_____

_____

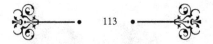

5 SENSES OF ABUNDANCE

We all have 5 senses of abundance, but do we all use them? Are you even aware of them? Let's have a look at what they are and how they can make a difference in how you live abundantly.

SIGHT

Are you looking through the eyes of abundance or the eyes of lack? For example, looking through the eyes of lack is to do you food shop and go straight to the 'reduced to clear' section without even thinking about it, or to choose the cheapest brand of everything without thinking about it.

Looking through the eyes of abundance is to just buy what you need and to choose the brand you want and not look at the cost. The results may surprise you as often you buy more of what you don't need just because it's cheap. Give it a try and see how good it makes you feel too.

If you are on a tight budget, treat your eyes to a feast of what you'd truly like and then reward your sense of abundance with one purchase of a little indulgent treat. Look through eyes of abundance!

HEARING

Do you listen through ears of lack or through ears of abundance? This will resonate with a lot of people. How often do you hear…

- ♥ Get a proper job!
- ♥ There's not enough money to go round!
- ♥ People with lots of money are always miserable!
- ♥ Spiritual people shouldn't charge for their services!

These are lack mindset words from people that are uncomfortable in making an effort to improve their own money story. Listen with ears of abundance to people who

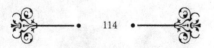

have made money themselves, people who will empower you and people who will help uplift you. Listen to words of positivity, not negativity.

Listen to women who are now amazing entrepreneurs in the online world. Focus on how different people's stories make you feel. Listen with ears of abundance.

SMELL

You may not have even considered smell as a sense of abundance. But believe me, it is! How often do you stop and smell fresh flowers? Flower essences can truly light up your sense of abundance.

How often do you take in the aroma of good food before you rush to eat it? Stop and enjoy the aroma of the food you enjoy. My favourite sense of smell for abundance is to wear my favourite perfume to bed. In doing this you are showing you truly are worthy of abundance.

SPEECH

How we speak about money massively affects us. It affects our money energy and our universal vibe too. Think about your money talk. Is it...

NEGATIVE TALK
Money doesn't like me.
I never have any money.
I'll never get out of debt.
People like me are never rich!

OR

POSITIVE TALK
Money loves me.
Money flows to me abundantly.

I am grateful that my debt reduces with each payment.

People like me are smashing their money goals and creating abundant lives!

The way we speak about ourselves and money can make a difference between success and failure. It affects our sense of self and our confidence. Listen to how you speak about money and speak through words of abundance!

TOUCH

This is one of my favourites. How is touch attached to abundance are you thinking? Well let's have a look, shall we!

When you go shopping for underwear do you go for Bridget Jones big baggy cottons? Or do you go for beautiful silk Bridget Bardot's that feel gorgeous next to your skin?

When you go clothes shopping do you head regularly into low-cost stores and grab a bargain whether you need it or not? Or do you go into an individual boutique and buy yourself a real treat occasionally?

Do you ever go into a jewellers shop and try on a really expensive piece of jewellery just to see how it feels?

Do you ever go into a car showroom and try the feel of the car you've always dreamed of?

Embrace the feeling of luxury and let your subconscious mind know you are ready for an amazing lifestyle. Feel the abundance.

TASTE

Taste is a wonderful way to embrace abundance and one you should treat yourself too regularly. Here's a little insight into it.

When you go out for food do you head for the nearest burger bar, pub grub or carvery? Or do you treat yourself to lunch in a bistro or scrumptious fine dining restaurants?

When shopping for wine do you buy one you really love

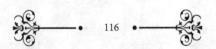

or do you go for a cheaper wine just to save a pound/dollar or two? I encourage you to pencil out a day in your diary just for you. Take yourself out for lunch. Avoid paper tablecloths and self-service. Treat yourself to table service and fine food with a glass of wine.

If you're not quite comfortable in lunching alone at least go out and treat yourself to a glass of champagne, just because you deserve it. Taste the abundance!

5 SENSES OF ABUNDANCE
JOURNALING TASK

Do I need to work on my 5 senses of abundance?

SIGHT

_____

_____

_____

_____

HEARING

_____

_____

_____

_____

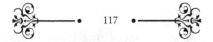

SMELL

_____

_____

_____

_____

_____

SPEECH

_____

_____

_____

_____

_____

TOUCH

_____

_____

_____

_____

_____

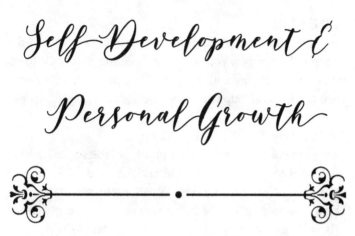

Self-Development & Personal Growth

*Be the Queen of your own thoughts,
not the slave.*

Every day should be a learning day and we should always seek to improve upon the skills we already have. It's not about impressing people it's about gaining knowledge, experience and communication that will help us gain more insights into how we can improve our mindset and creative gifts. This, in turn, will increase our money flow!

READ BOOKS

There are tons of self-development books to choose from now. Treat yourself and fully immerse yourself. If you have a busy schedule aim to read at least 2 chapters a day, otherwise, you'll keep putting off reading. Put your feet up and read!

MENTORS AND COACHES

Find somebody that inspires you. There is a lot of free mentoring accessible online through books and videos. But it's important to invest in you. Free stuff will only take you so far. Investing in yourself is the best investment you will ever make.

COURSES

I'm a great believer in doing free courses to find your niche interest. Then when you have the direction you want to go invest in expert paid courses that will stretch your knowledge even further and help you grow. Every day is a learning day.

PASSION IS A KEY TO SUCCESS

Passion is a truly great starter point for true success. I have a friend who is passionate about antiques and coffee. So she opened a coffee shop and filled it with antique furniture and china. Everything was for sale as well as the coffee and cakes!

If you have one or two passions you can usually make a business out of them. Even better today is the fact you can open a worldwide online shop without having to pay ridiculous overheads as you do for a physical shop in the real world. In an online shop, the whole world is your customer. And with the amazing progress within social media, you can sell on many different platforms.

Saleable knowledge is increasingly a big seller and is only set to get bigger. Interestingly it is predominantly women entrepreneurs that have fully grasped this knowledge, taken it on board and are making some serious money from it.

What's saleable knowledge you might be thinking? Well, let's look at the most successful business first of all. Life Coaching. This is a business that can be done through strategy calls, facetime, workbooks and so on. But increasingly the area of saleable knowledge is spreading into all different types of coaching such as business mentoring, manifesting, self-love, body confidence or nutrition.

Think about what saleable knowledge you have. Are you a chef? You can sell delicious recipes for all palates, cooking on a budget or children's recipes.

Are you a jewellery maker? You can sell workshops or courses on how to make necklaces or bracelets. Create a pack

on different gems, what they ar,e where they come from and where to buy them.

Are you an animal lover? You could sell pet care packs, behaviour guides, or even holistic healing for animals.

The flame of passion can light up the world!

SELF DEVELOPMENT & PERSONAL GROWTH JOURNALING TASK

What are your passions that you could turn into an opportunity?

_____

_____

_____

_____

_____

_____

_____

_____

_____

_____

Moonology

Child of the stars, essence of the Universe.

The energy of the moon is both beautiful and magical. And don't let anyone ever tell you it isn't! There are many ways the moon affects our daily lives. You probably know a few already such as farmers planting crops according to moon cycles. Or that the word 'lunatic' comes from the Latin word for the moon Luna. The fact that more babies are born on a full moon and that a full moon can start a romance!

A lot of people can feel their energy shift around a full moon for a few days. The two main moons to familiarise yourself with are the full moon and the new moon.

THE FULL MOON

The full moon is a time for releasing anything which no longer serves you. Sometimes you can feel out of sorts around the full moon, this is the natural pull of the moon's energy.

You may feel drawn to water, especially if you are a spiritual person. This is also natural and relates to the ebb and flow of the tides around the full moon. If you feel drawn to the ocean, then go, it will help you feel renewed.

A simple full moon releasing ritual is to write a list of whatever it is you feel you want to let go of, take it outside and burn it under the moonlight.

Then have yourself a gorgeous bathing ceremony to cleanse

yourself, also dipping your head fully underwater to cut any negative energy threads that may still be attached to you.

Here's another ritual you can enjoy:

FULL MOON MILK BATH
250ml organic almond milk.
1 handful of pink Himalayan salt
1 handful of rose petals
5 drops lavender oil
5 drops rose oil
Place moonstone and selenite crystals around your bathing area.
Run hot water in the bath.
Add the salt crystals while the bath is filling, allowing to dissolve before you get in.
Then add the almond milk, rose petals and essential oil.
Light your favourite candle, put on some gentle music and spend some time relaxing and focus what you would like to release with the full moon energy.

NEW MOON
The new moon brings a different type of energy. It brings a refreshing energy and a time of new beginnings. The new moon is a great time to set your intentions for what you would like the universe to bring you.

It's best to set your intentions when you are in a positive mindset, so do a little releasing meditation before making your list of intentions and setting them with a prayer or crystals if you like.

The new moon is also a good one to not only set your intentions with words but also with images too. Why not create a new moon vision board?

Find some gorgeous images of the moon and create your list of wishes and dreams you'd like to achieve with the help

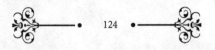

of la luna. You could place this outside with your crystals so it can soak up the magic of the moonbeams. Go big with your wishes and dreams and let your imagination flow with love and gratitude.

FULL MOON NAMES

JANUARY
Known as The Wolf Moon or Fox Moon.

FEBRUARY
Known as The Snow Moon or Hunger Moon

MARCH
Known as The Worm Moon or Crow Moon

APRIL
Known as The Pink Moon or Grass Moon

MAY
Known as The Flower Moon or Corn Moon

JUNE
Known as The Rose Moon, Flower Moon or Strawberry Moon

JULY
Known as The Thunder Moon or Buck Moon

AUGUST
Known as The Sturgeon Moon

SEPTEMBER
Known as The Harvest Moon

OCTOBER
Known as The Blue Moon or The Hunter's Moon

NOVEMBER
Known as The Frosty Moon or Beaver Moon

DECEMBER
Known as The Cold Moon

MOONOLOGY
JOURNALING TASK

List what you would like to release on the next full moon

_____

_____

_____

_____

_____

_____

_____

_____

List what you would like to call in from the universe on the next new moon

_____

_____

_____

_____

_____

_____

_____

_____

_____

_____

_____

_____

_____

_____

_____

_____

_____

Self-Love

Be the one you love.

Love is all and everlasting. It is the ultimate gift that increases when passed on for both the giver and the receiver. Love always starts with God and ourselves.

Self-love is one of the most important subjects for moving forward on a happy and successful journey for everyone. We can become so distracted with other people's opinions rather than the one that matters the most, our own! Self-love is essential for happiness and success in life and it starts with your own thoughts and the way you talk to yourself.

Self-talk is the ultimate gift you have that can help you live your best life. When talking to yourself don't say anything that you wouldn't say to your best friend or a truly loved one. Self-talk should be loving, caring, uplifting and most of all empowering!

It's also important to treat yourself, take yourself out on a 'date day!' Go out to lunch, a little glass of champagne is guaranteed to make you feel good about yourself! Buy yourself something, it doesn't have to be mega expensive even a new notebook or flowers will empower you.

Stay away from 'ninja whingers!' – we all have them in our life. They want to use you as an emotional prop for their own anxieties. Well guess what, that's not your responsibility.

If you can't avoid being in the presence of a negative person then just bear witness to what they are saying but don't take it on emotionally. That's just their opinion; it has nothing to do with you. The more you learn to do this the easier it will become. Arm yourself with some great books too that will increase your sense of self and grow your confidence. Fall in love with yourself.

LOVE JAR RECIPE

Here's a little treat you can make for yourself to attract and grow your own vibration of love.

WHAT YOU WILL NEED

Himalayan pink salt
Dried orange rind
Dried rosemary
1 dried red rose

Place the jar near your front door to welcome love into your home. Layer all the ingredients with the rose facing outward. Refresh the ingredients every 3-6 months.

SELF LOVE JOURNALING
TASK

List the things you love about yourself

_____

_____

_____

_____

_____

List the love gifts you are going to treat yourself to

_____

_____

_____

_____

_____

_____

_____

_____

_____

_____

_____

_____

_____

_____

_____

_____

_____

_____

_____

Manifesting

Have faith in yourself and trust in the Universe.

Manifesting has grown in popularity in recent years as people come to realise they do have an ability to call in their dream life.

The secret to it is… You are the one who holds the only magic secret when it comes to manifesting! It's all about your vibration and the energy you choose for it. A positive vibration will bring positive energy. A negative vibration will bring negative energy. So make sure you're tuned into the right vibrational energy. It's your choice. Let's look at what you need to succeed in manifesting.

THOUGHTS

'Thoughts become things.' This is true. Which is why it is important to keep your mindset as positive as you can. No one can be 100% positive 24 hours a day. But finding the right balance is key to manifesting.

FEELINGS

There is absolutely no point in thinking positive thoughts if you don't truly believe them in your heart and soul. Your thoughts are just empty words otherwise.

If you are thinking 'I am so excited about what's coming for me and I can't wait to embrace it'. But in your heart, you are feeling the usual a sense of lack or fear you are telling yourself the right energy cannot connect with you. You always have to come from a place of love and gratitude in your heart when manifesting. You just need to practice making a shift in your energy.

How do you do that?
- ♥ Journaling
- ♥ Self-development
- ♥ Being around positive people
- ♥ Vision Boards
- ♥ Love Boards
- ♥ Meditation
- ♥ Crystal energy

THOUGHTS & FEELINGS JOURNALING TASK

How can you improve upon your thoughts and feelings when manifesting?

_____

_____

_____

_____

_____

_____

INSPIRED ACTION

The first inspired action anyone should be taking is clearing your space so your energy can flow! Decluttering is essential. Have a massive clear-out. Your home, garage, attic, kitchen, bathroom, living space, bedroom, wardrobe, handbags and even your purse. No old receipts, business cards, buttons cluttering up your precious money space!

Keep a manifesting inspired action journal. Divide each page into two. On one side write what you would like to manifest.On the other write the inspired action you can take to help the universe in making it happen.

For instance, if you would like a new house your inspired action would be: buy a new keyring for the key to your new house.

If you want a new car your inspired action would be: Go and test drive and choose the colour of your dream car.

If you want to have a holiday in the country of your dreams your inspired action would be: Place that countries currency in your purse so the universe gets the message that's where you want to go!

INSPIRED ACTION
JOURNALING TASK

Which inspired actions can you take to bring in what you truly want?

_____

_____

_____

_____

_____

_____

_____

_____

_____

_____

_____

_____

GRATITUDE

For me, this is as important as your vibrational energy. Gratitude is everything! If you're not thankful for what you receive then why should you receive more? Your day should start with thanks.

- ♥ Thanks for a good night's sleep.
- ♥ Thanks for another beautiful day to be alive.
- ♥ Thanks for the amazing people in my life.
- ♥ Thanks for the nourishing food I am able to eat.
- ♥ Bless all your food!

Once you understand the power of gratitude you will be even more thankful!

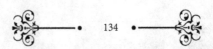

GRATITUDE JOURNALING
TASK

What are you grateful for?

_____

_____

_____

_____

_____

_____

_____

_____

_____

_____

_____

_____

_____

_____

_____

_____

_____

MANIFESTING BY NUMBERS

This is massive when you fully understand the power of it. Numerology is an essential part of working with manifesting. Each day brings its own gift through number vibration. If you are an 8 you are a naturally gifted manifester. 1 and 11 also bring success and 11 brings a message of opportunity to manifest by. Working with numerology within manifesting is a joy when you understand it.

CRYSTALS

There are many crystals whose energy will enhance your manifesting skills. These are 3 of my favourites

Citrine. A great crystal for calling in your dreams

Pyrite. Amazing for improving your money mindset

Clear Quartz. A great conductor for bringing in energy. I could go on about manifesting for literally hours or even days! But that gives you some basic ideas. Let's look now at different methods available for manifesting.

555 MANIFESTING CHALLENGE

555 is a way of training your subconscious mind into a manifesting state.

You have to be committed to doing this challenge and stick to it. To do this challenge choose one thing you want to manifest and turn it into an affirmation. You have to put it as if you already have it and use the RIGHT WORDS in your affirmation.

I HAVE

I WILL

I AM

I LOVE

For instance, you could choose a new bag. You could write your affirmation as 'I am grateful that I have my new bag. It is truly beautiful and I love it.' Now here is what you have to

do to train your subconscious mind into a state of openness for manifesting energy.

You have to write out your affirmation 55 times a day for 5 days. You have to write in in capital letters to emphasise its energy. You can split it into sections but you have to do it 55 times a day. Give it a go and see what you can manifest!

METHODICAL MANIFESTING JOURNALING TASKS

Which additional methods can you add to your manifesting skills?

_____

_____

_____

_____

_____

_____

_____

_____

_____

_____

ANGEL GUIDANCE WITH MANIFESTING

Angels are divine spiritual beings of love and light that work with us throughout our lifetime. They can bring us messages, guidance and help for our highest good. Angels work with the spiritual laws of the universe, which means that the angels will not directly interfere in your life unless you ask them to.

When you ask for guidance, your angels will guide you with messages, signs and through working with your intuition. You may also receive what are known as downloads. This is when your angels give you guidance in a collective thought or inspiration. These are sometimes instant and can give you a 'wow' moment!

When you ask your angels directly for help with something, you create a connection of guidance. Our angels can help us with manifesting in most areas of our life. This does not mean that if you ask for a million-pound house it will magically appear! That is not how it works. Can you imagine the chaos if it did?

Think of it this way, if your best friend needed help with something but you knew they needed to figure it out for themselves, you would help them with advice, guidance and support. This is the same way our angels help us with manifesting because the experience of learning is valuable for bringing the right results at the right time.

When we ask our angels for help in manifesting something it should always be for our highest and greater good. Manifesting should always be done with love and gratitude in your heart and always from a place of light. Then our angels can work with us by sending us inspiration, ideas, signs, opportunities, helpers, and also through synchronicities and serendipity. This helps bring our dreams into reality. All we have to do is act upon the inspirations, ideas and signs we receive. We cannot just sit back and wait for it to happen. We

have to take inspired action. Here are some ways in which your angels can help you with manifesting.

IDEAS AND INSPIRATIONS

As mentioned it's so important when you receive inspirations to take action upon them. A common mistake people make is thinking that these ideas and inspirations are crazy and don't follow the guidance. Never doubt the guidance you receive as it can truly lead you to the magic.

OPPORTUNITY

How many times have you heard 'when opportunity knocks, you need to answer!' When you ask the angels for help, you may find new areas of opportunity open up for you. This can sometimes be brought about by synchronicity too. It's important to be aware of this and not just watch these opportunities pass by. Always take inspired action when there is an aligned opening for you. The most common problem people have is taking action.

Sometimes all that is required for success is to spread your wings and fly. Don't sit twiddling your thumbs or whispering ifs and buts to yourself. Doing this will lead to opportunities passing you by and often not returning at all.

BE SPECIFIC

Being specific on what you want an important key to manifesting. Your angels need clarity to help you achieve your dreams.

Sometimes we can worry about being too specific because of fear that we won't achieve what we want. But sometimes we just need to get out of our own way. Your angels will encourage and guide you towards your bigger goals. They can help you grow in self-confidence too so you are brave enough to truly step up into your dream life.

Focus on what you want and let your angels guide you towards it. If you want to call in your dream house put your energy fully into it. Be specific about each room, what will the windows face onto? What will the garden look like? What colour will the front door be? What will be the layout of the bathroom and bedrooms? Your angels can help you if they have a clearer picture of what you want.

ASKING YOUR ANGELS FOR HELP

Asking your angels for help isn't complicated. The best way to do this is to come from a place of love and gratitude in your heart, not from a place of lack or desperation. Surrendering up to your Angels for help is one of the most amazing experiences to have. It can make you feel truly lighter too. All you need to do is ask! A great way to ask is simply by saying 'I AM READY'.

Opening up to guidance is so much easier than you may think. Be aware of any inspirations, signs or messages you receive. You may also find new people entering your life who are there to help you achieve your dreams.

Then be sure to take inspired action to bring about the results you want. And most of all don't forget to be grateful for what you receive.

VISION BOARDS

Using a vision board can truly help you by bringing joy to your heart each time you look at it and add to it, this, in turn, raises your vibration. Understanding the guidance we can receive from angels and what they can help us with is key to bringing our visions into reality. An angel vision board is not only helpful to us but is a beautiful creation to look at too.

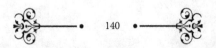

MANIFESTING WITH ANGELS JOURNALING TASKS

List the ways in which you can work with your angels to help you when you're manifesting

_____

_____

_____

_____

_____

_____

_____

_____

_____

_____

_____

_____

_____

_____

_____

_____

The Celestial Divines

Allow yourself to be guided by love.

The more you travel on your journey of spirituality the more the magic reveals itself to you. I love learning about the planets, their energies, their connection to angels and the true majesty of the universe. The sun, moon and Venus are what I like to call the celestial divines because of the beautiful magic they bring us.

SUN

The sun is a beautiful ball of fire shining for the entire world to see. Michael is the archangel of the sun. There's no coincidence his main guidance influence is on his day Sunday. The sun brings us warmth, strength and light. These are also the gifts Michael wants to bring us. He can help us receive light and inspiration and cut negative cords from us. He can also help us find strength and confidence through his ball of fire, much like the Sun.

Another archangel connected to the sun is archangel Zadkiel is also associated with the sun. A beautiful golden angel of abundance who can help us shine to our true potential if we take the opportunity to spread our wings and fly.

Within numerology, the life path numbers connected to the sun are 1 and 3. Flowers associated with the sun and abundance are sunflowers and marigolds. Crystals associated with the sun are carnelian, tigers eye and yellow jasper.

MOON

The moon has always had a magical pull, especially for women. Whilst men try and conquer its craters and stick their flags in it, women focus on understanding its magical energy force. We flow energetically with the moon cycles and tides. We connect with the romance of the moon.

Archangel Gabriel is the angel of the moon. He is known as the ruler of the Moon, which incidentally gives us Moonday Monday. Monday is also Archangel Gabriel's main guidance influence day and a day to focus on and grow your own intuition. Pearls have an association with the moon too. This is no surprise as water is heavily connected with the moon too as our oceans reflect its energy in their tidal flow. No wonder why we love pearls so much too!

The moon shows us wherever there is darkness there will always be light. The numbers 369 have long been associated with the moon. Nikola Tesla said 'If you only understood the significance of the 369 you would have the key to the universe.' I think he understood the magic of the moon too.

It never ceases to amaze me when I see the way the angels align themselves with moons during the calendar year. We are literally bombarded with guidance and magic but only those open to receiving will see it.

Life path numbers associated with the moon are 7 and 11. Crystals associated with the moon are moonstone and labradorite. Flowers associated with the moon are jasmine and honeysuckle.

VENUS

Venus, 'the bright morning star,' 'the loving evening star.' Venus has guided us with her beautiful bounty of love and abundance from the beginning of time. In relation to religion, venus is highly significant. Jesus is mentioned in nearly all religion as the son of God, a messiah, prophet and spiritual leader. The magi (3 wise men or kings) were professional astronomers and astrologers. They identified the star that led them to the birth of Jesus as venus. They witnessed the venus rose as she went through her rebirth into a morning star. This is when Venus is in abundance. Light is abundant.

The world received a message in abundance with the birth of Jesus. Jesus is said to describe himself as 'the bright morning star' in the book of revelation.

The archangels associated with Venus are archangel Haniel and archangel Uriel. Both are angels of love. Archangel Uriel's guidance influence is on a Friday. When Venus is a night star she is guiding us to focus on love and relationships. Love brings light into darkness. Venus is our constant reminder of this. Life path numbers associated with Venus are 6 and 9. Flowers associated with Venus are roses and peonies. Crystals associated with Venus are rose quartz, snow quartz, pink opal and rhodochrosite.

CELESTIAL WATERS

You can charge up beautiful celestial waters for use in bathing or rituals for releasing, cleansing, love and abundance too.

To make celestial waters you will need:

A clean screw-top jar

Filtered water

Crystals and flowers of your choice

Place the jar of filtered water under your chosen divine celestial. Place your crystals on top of the jar and

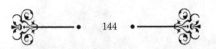

surround it with your flowers. You can place a list or letter under your water that you'd like help with if you wish. Leave for 12 -24 hours before using.

SUN WATER

Leave out in the sunlight for as long as it lasts. For strength and self-confidence ask Archangel Michael for guidance whilst charging your water. For abundance, you can ask Archangel Zadkiel for help.

MOON WATER

Leave under the moonlight for releasing with a new moon or calling in your dreams with a new moon. You can also ask archangel Gabriel for guidance whilst charging your water.

VENUS WATER

When Venus is in her 'evening star' this is the phase for self-love and relationships. You can also ask archangel Uriel and archangel Haniel to help whilst charge your water. Enjoy your Celestial Divine waters!

CELESTIAL DIVINES
JOURNALING TASK

Which of the celestial divines do you feel most drawn too and why?

_____

_____

_____

The Elements

To truly know yourself is enlightening.

The elements with their energy and vibration allow us to wonderfully connect to the magic of the universe. Here are some insights into the magic of the elements.

WATER

Water carries the energy of the feminine awakening that women are currently experiencing. Water has patience, inner strength and persistence.

Consider water and a stone, you may think the stone is stronger. But over time a single drop of water hitting a stone can create an indentation in the stone. Water shows us that being patient and persistence we can forge a strong path, even one that others can follow.

Water is cleansing and purifying and we can embrace this when we need to let go of what doesn't serve us. We can do this by bathing or showering and imagining cutting negative cords away from us.

WATER – SPIRITUAL ENERGY ZONE
The magic pull of the sea can be felt deep in your soul and can fill you emotionally at times with joy and at other times with a longing or a long-forgotten sadness or loss.

The sea is a place of mystery and magic. We hear so many mythical stories of sea monsters, pirates and sailors lost at sea. But the legend that has roots in all cultures around the world is the tales of mermaids or sirens. We have an endless fascination with them. The song of the siren has its own poignancy. We are made up mainly of water and women flow with the energy of the moon, so it's no surprise really why we find the sea so fascinating.

THE MAGICAL ELEMENT
OF WATER

WATER PLANETS
Moon
Neptune
Pluto

THE ARCHANGELS OF WATER
Archangel Gabriel
Archangel Michael

ZODIAC WATER SIGNS
Cancer
Scorpio
Pisces

WATER PERSONALITIES
Intuitive
Emotional
Mysterious
Psychic
Sensitive and loving

WATER SENSE

Taste: The simplest of all tastes is water But it is essential to life for us isn't it. I do believe as you grow through a spiritual awakening you drink more water. I find as well I receive most of my guidance when I'm near water.

WATER CRYSTALS
Clear Quartz
Selenite
Aquamarine
'You are water whirling water
Yet still trapped within
Come submerge yourself within us
We who are the flowing stream.' – Rumi

EARTH

Earth gives us life itself. Mother Nature or Gaia encourages life to spring forth from her with love. The earth grounds, holds and supports us.

It carries us through the seasons time after time. It brings us food from its roots and also heals us from its many plants and herbs.

There is no time like the present when we should be paying attention to how we treat the beautiful earth we have. We should cherish the gifts it gives us and reward its nurturing in turn with love and compassion. A lesson sadly many of us still have yet to learn.

EARTH – SPIRITUAL ENERGY ZONE
How fabulous does it feel to kick your shoes off and walk barefoot in the grass, or to throw your arms around a tree and

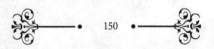

give it a loving hug. Connecting with the earth is a beautiful way to connect with your angels too.

How much magic do we associate with the earth? In the 16th century, an alchemist named Parcelus wrote a book called 'Philosophia Magna' in which he wrote about fairies, sprites, elves and other mythical creatures.

He described writing the book to 'describe creatures outside of the light of nature, beings between creature and spirit.' He truly understood the magic of the earth!

THE MAGICAL ELEMENT OF EARTH

EARTH PLANETS
Venus
Saturn

THE ARCHANGELS OF EARTH
Archangel Sandalphon
Archangel Raphael

ZODIAC EARTH SIGNS
Taurus
Virgo
Capricorn

EARTH PERSONALITIES
Nurturing
Supportive
Considerate
Relaxed

EARTH SENSE

Smell: How blessed are we to receive the beautiful smell of flowers gifted to us from the earth. For me, the smell of wet soil on a moonlit night carries its own magic too especially for recharging your crystals by placing them in it overnight.

EARTH CRYSTALS
Hematite
Malachite
Aragonite

'And into the forest, I go to lose
My mind and find my soul.' – Anon

AIR

Air has its own magical energy. We often refer to people as a 'breathe of fresh air.' We also look at the northwind as a bringer of magic and mystical energies. It is believed that romance is blown in by charmed winds and air is also essential to life for enabling us to breathe. There are lots of breath exercises you can do to fill up your soul too.

AIR – SPIRITUAL ENERGY ZONE

Air spiritual energy zones are usually found in mountains or on a high hilltop. It's an exhilarating feeling when you stand with the earth beneath your feet and nothing above you but the sky. Breathing in fresh air deeply can help you feel truly connected and aligned with the Universe.

Running against the wind on a hilltop is amazing. You can truly feel the force of nature when you do this. And it's a great way to cleanse oneself. Allow the wind to blow away

your cobwebs! Even sitting with your eyes closed in a gentle breeze will make you feel renewed and connected.

THE MAGICAL ELEMENT OF AIR

AIR PLANETS
Mercury
Uranus
Jupiter

THE ARCHANGELS OF AIR
Archangel Raphael
Archangel Haniel

ZODIAC AIR SIGNS
Gemini
Libra
Aquarius

AIR PERSONALITIES
Brave
Intelligent
Restless
Bohemian

AIR SENSE
Hearing: Who listens to the whispers of the wind. I love to do this and believe it's a beautiful way to connect with Angels and Spirit. Listen closely on a windy day and hear the gentle whispers of the wind. Let the magic swirl around you through the gifts of nature.

AIR CRYSTALS

Green Aventurine
Topaz
Amber
'Born of wind
I am free
Spiritual brave and wise.' – Anon

FIRE

Fire has been with us since the beginning of time through the energy of the sun. We first discovered how to create it for ourselves right back at the beginning of mankind and we have been entranced with it ever since.

Flame readers are people that have an ability to 'see' in the flames of fire or in the smoke of candles. As I've mentioned, my nana was a flame reader. I remember she knew when someone was coming to see her because she saw them in the flames before they arrived.

Fire can also protect us. We have always built fires out in the open at night to keep us safe. When we are connecting with archangel Michael we can ask him to fill us with strength and confidence from his ball of fire. We use fire to describe people as 'hot-headed' or as a description 'flaming red hair.' Fire has and always will draw us in with its own magic.

FIRE – SPIRITUAL ENERGY ZONE

The spiritual energy zone of fire draws us to vast desserts and under the beauty and power of the sun. Many wise men, shamans and magi's have made their way to the desert to connect with their own spiritual magic.

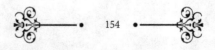

Fire circles are a way many people choose to connect spiritually too. It's often a way to share experiences and stories from ages past too.

THE MAGICAL ELEMENT OF FIRE

FIRE PLANETS
Sun
Mars

THE ARCHANGELS OF FIRE
Archangel Michael

ZODIAC FIRE SIGNS
Aries
Leo
Sagittarius

FIRE PERSONALITIES
Courageous
Strong
Steadfast
Enthusiastic
Fearless

FIRE SENSE
Sight: 'Look into the flames' is a term I connect with an ability to 'see' clearly. Sight has been long connected with psychic abilities. It is discovering our own fire within us that gives us the courage to be 'seen' as we truly are. Shine

like the sun and never lose 'sight' of your true desires.
Be the flame that ignites someone else's fire too!

FIRE CRYSTALS
  Fire Opal
  Red Jasper
  Tigers Eye

'Stop acting small
You are the universe
In ecstatic motion
Set your life on fire
Seek those who can fan your flames.' – Rumi

THE ELEMENTS
JOURNALING TASK

Which of the elements are you most drawn too? List how
connecting with this element has helped you and makes you
feel.

_____

_____

_____

_____

_____

_____

Spiritual Journaling

Let stuff go. Love your flow!

I always recommend spiritual journaling. It's amazing to see your thoughts from starting and where you are currently. It's often a joy to look back on and see how you've grown and the amazing insights you've discovered along the way!

It is a place where you can record your first spiritual awakening experience.

What may have brought you to it? How you felt about it at the time. How you feel about it now. The insights you've had along the way. The messages, signs and connections you've had. The crystals you have chosen and have helped you. The angels you've connected with and had guidance from. It is an ongoing journal that will grow with you and be such a useful record for you to refer to and look back on.

This may be the beginning of a new journey for you. In which case you are in exactly the right place in starting your journal so you can record all your experiences that will help you on the start of a beautiful journey. Every journey starts with the first step.

THE BEGINNING

What was it that brought you to this point? The thought,

happening or insight that sparked the start of your journey? Whatever it was this should be your first entry into your journal. Share what it was, when it happened and how you felt about it.

If you haven't had an actual spiritual awakening sign yet but are open to receiving one, write down how you feel and what you are looking for. Being open to receiving is one of the easiest ways for it to happen. Connecting with nature in woodland, fields, by the sea or by a stream are all ways to find that wonderful connection. You can also simply ask in prayer for a sign or guidance and listen in meditation for an answer or guidance. Always come from a place of love and gratitude in your heart.

SPIRIT SPIRITUAL SPACES

You can create your spiritual space anywhere. It doesn't matter whether it's a single shelf to a whole room. It's your space to create as you wish.

Create a special place where you can be at one with yourself, your crystals, totems, journals and most of all your angels.

It should be a place to spend time in thought and meditation when possible. It's a place to store the sentimental items that bring you joy, happiness, love and gratitude.

You can create a space wherever you are. Create one in a corner when visiting friends and relatives. Create a beautiful one on a beach when you are on holiday - these are especially nice to do if you are on a retreat holiday.

You can also create them outdoors in a garden where you can sit in nature and really enjoy your journaling. Connecting with nature is one of the most wonderful ways to connect with your angels.

It is also a lovely way to feel the energy of nature around you so that it can help you journal about how it feels. It's your space to enjoy and be loved!

HIGHER SELF JOURNALING

Once you are universally awake you may be eager to move forward with your new-found you! One of the best ways to achieve a successful mindset is to higher self journal. Higher self journaling is you as your higher self. Journal it in the now, not as your future self.

How do you dress?

Which perfume do you wear?

How is your hair styled?

Which career have you chosen?

Where do you live?

What does your house look like?

Where do you travel?

What do you do for the benefit of others?

Journal every morning whenever possible. This will set your vibrational energy for the day. *Breathe in the magic!*

INTUITION

One of the most common spiritual awakening experiences is a heightened intuition and in some cases the realisation that you have a psychic gift.

An important factor to note here is to keep yourself fully grounded and your energy protected. A simple way to do this is by always grounding yourself before doing any energy work. You can use hematite and a simple meditation for this.

For protection use an amethyst when using energy work so you don't take on any client energy. This also helps prevent any fatigue or tiredness you can pick up.

It is also important not to get sidetracked onto the wrong path. Energy is incredibly powerful so make sure you always work with light and don't enter into any dark energy work.

Always come from a place of love in your heart and trust in your intuition.

If you're not sure about something, ask, there are plenty of

spiritual women who will be more than happy to help you.

JOURNALING IS A JOY!

Don't put any pressure on yourself that it has to be neat or in your best handwriting! Just enjoy making your entries. You can place any feathers you may find between the pages or even dried flower petals to give it an extra special touch.

SPIRITUAL JOURNALING TASK

Start your journal and over the next few months see in which areas you feel you have grown the most.

_____

_____

_____

_____

_____

_____

_____

_____

_____

_____

_____

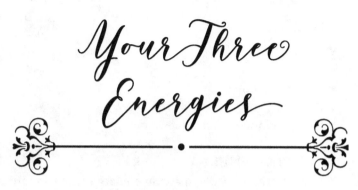

Your Three Energies

Let your eyes see what your soul feels.

Some people go through life without even realising they have these energies. Some people are aware of one or two of them but not everyone is aware of all of them and how we can create magic by flowing with them.

These 3 energies are known as feminine, masculine and spirit.

Understanding how we work through them is easy and not complicated at all really. Getting the balance working with these energies makes life so much easier too.

The two energies most people are aware of is the feminine and masculine energy. Not everyone is aware of their spirit energy or that they even use it. But it's our spirit energy that can truly help us live our best life. Let's look at the energies and how you can embrace them.

FEMININE ENERGY

You are working in your feminine energy whenever we are creating, inspiring and working emotionally. Here are just some examples of when you are in your feminine energy.

- ♥ Writing or speaking inspirationally
- ♥ Using your imagination
- ♥ Daydreaming

- ♥ Nurturing
- ♥ Sharing love
- ♥ Singing
- ♥ Supporting others
- ♥ Reflecting
- ♥ Sharing kindness and compassion

MASCULINE ENERGY

You are working in our masculine energy when we are doing, planning and taking action. Here are just some examples of when you are working in your masculine energy.

- ♥ Creating a to-do list
- ♥ Taking inspired action on any ideas you have
- ♥ Decision making
- ♥ Taking a risk
- ♥ Focusing on a goal
- ♥ Thinking logically
- ♥ Analysing
- ♥ Asserting
- ♥ Taking the lead

SPIRIT ENERGY

This is the energy that people are awakening to and working with. Working with your spirit energy is not to be confused with working purely as a medium or just working with your Clair gifts. Everyone can work in their spirit energy. Here are just some examples of when you are working in your spirit energy.

- ♥ Connecting with your angels
- ♥ Praying
- ♥ Practising Meditation
- ♥ Working with your crystal energy
- ♥ Spiritual learning
- ♥ Working with your intuition or sixth sense

- ♥ Using your Clair gifts
- ♥ Connecting with spirit or your spirit guides
- ♥ Healing

Finding and working in balance with all these energies is a beautiful way to live. We can't expect to be in one energy all of the time. What do I mean by this? Well, here's an experience I had with one of my clients.

My client was stressed because she had been on a roll with one of her spirit guides bringing guidance through for her. Then she had no connection at all for a few days and was panicking thinking she'd lost her ability to connect and also her gifts of clairvoyance and clairaudience. But I explained to her that you can't be in the same energy 100% of the time or you would crash and burn. You have to work through all of your energies inflow.

And sure enough, a few days later she was connecting and working in her spirit energy again. The universe wants you to be in flow with all of your energies so you can truly live your best life! Learn to flow in alignment with all that you are and life will lead you on a journey of wonderment.

THREE ENERGIES JOURNALING TASK

How ccan you balance working in your three energies more?

_____

_____

_____

_____

Divine Feminine Sisters

Lift others with love.

No matter who you are, where you're from and no matter whatever your education or background, you have a gift to bring to the world.

I find working with numerology helps me find the light within so many. It has helped me see the divine feminine energy within everyone. I have looked at each life path number and its essence of the universe.

It has through this insightful knowledge that I have been able to share the following divine feminine sister energies that we share worldwide.

We are all blessed with light within us that we can share with others and here you will find a key to what your light is.

LIFE PATH 1 – THE INDEPENDENT LEADER

Your divine feminine sister energy: the prophetess of true power.

Your guidance is to show that we have the power to create the life we truly want for ourselves.

Your divine feminine story: You have echoes from ancient times that 'how you live your life is up to you!' We all have a divine will within us that is aligned with our soul purpose.

Yours is one of fierce strength and independence. You have the ability to bring that inner strength to others. Do not let others try and take your true power away from you. Let the fire of your own source be your strength!

Your divine feminine gift: you have the true gift of leadership. You can set the example for others to follow by living with the truth of your gifts and creating the life you fiercely desire.

Your soul chant: I own my power from the existence of all time.

Your soul voice message: lead from your inner strength of absolute trust.

Your essence intention: to empower sisters around the world to embrace their own strength and independence.

LIFE PATH 2 – THE PEACEFUL ONE

Your divine feminine sister energy: the mystic of peace.

Your guidance is to show that stillness in ourselves in any given moment can bring clarity and balance to our mind and energy.

Your divine feminine story: the universe shows us that we cannot solve problems with the same thoughts we used to create them. You have a beautiful ability to bring a sense of clarity and balance to others. You can help others see both sides of stories and bring a new understanding of how to find serenity within ourselves.

Your divine feminine gift: you have the ability to soften the chaos within others and to help bring calm and harmony to their being.

Your soul chant: I am peace. When my mind is clear, my path is clear.

Your soul voice message: from my heart, I will help you experience stillness, harmony and peace.

Your essence intention: to show that happiness is found within ourselves and not within the energy of others.

LIFE PATH 3 – THE CREATIVE EXPRESSIONIST

Your divine feminine sister energy: the creator of spoken words. Your guidance is to show it does not matter where your start in life begins it is your own truth and word that will define you.

Your divine feminine story: to show how we are the author of our own story. It is our voice that should shape the words that we speak and not the voice of others. You have a beautiful inner child energy that will not only be a guiding shining light for yourself but for others too. You are gifted with creativity, charisma and communication. It is a soul mission for you to share your gifts with the world. Let your magical energy shine through!

Your divine feminine gift: you are the creator of spoken light.

Your soul chant: I am a poet and artist of the inner child.

Your soul voice message: speak in your own creativity of truth.

Your essence intention: to lead through the joy of the creative energy.

LIFE PATH 4 – THE DEDICATED WORKER

Your divine feminine sister energy: the goddess of sanctuary.

Your guidance is no matter where you are, you are home. Sanctuary is always found within ourselves.

Your divine feminine story: you possess within you a soul power of strength and grounding energy that you can comfort others with. You are the rock that people will find strength in when they feel lost. You bring a sense of stability and comfort to all who find you.

You are generous and warmhearted. You have the ability to achieve all your life goals through dedication and perseverance. You have a grounded money energy that can be built upon for success. Dedication

should start within you for your own journey then given as a gift to others too.

Your divine feminine gift: I will help others find success through order and stability.

Your soul chant: I am a giver of sanctuary, strength and dedication.

Your soul voice message: we need to find stability when faced with the energy of chaos.

Your essence intention: to bring the energy of order and discipline to calm and make others feel safe.

LIFE PATH 5 – THE FREE ONE

Your divine feminine sister energy: the queen of possibilities.

Your guidance is to bring the realisation of free spirit and possibilities to all.

Your divine feminine story: it is essential to believe in your own true self and not what others believe you are capable of. You have the ability to prove that we can all achieve our dreams. We just need to smash through the glass ceilings our ego builds above our heads.

The possibilities of our soul's energy are limitless. You have the power of being a groundbreaker and trailblazer. You can achieve new heights of success that many others would not even try. Don't be held back by the restrictions of others. Live your dream life on your own terms!

Your divine feminine gift: I empower the energy of true possibility to others.

Your soul chant: I can create limitless success for myself.

Your soul voice message: to bring the energy of freedom and courage.

Your essence intention: to be the guiding light of true possibilities and vision.

LIFE PATH 6 – THE CARING ONE

Your divine feminine sister energy: Queen of the outsiders.

Your guidance is to lead with wherever you are whoever you're with, to embrace all with love.

Your divine feminine story: you are a queen of expressing the joy of self-love to all. Know there is nothing you need to prove or wait to become. There is only one deep abiding truth and that is love. You are and always have been truly loved. Love will give you the strength to grow and achieve whatever you strive for. You have the gift of love to give from your caring and beautiful heart. Love is your true power. Let it fill your soul.

Your divine feminine gift: you have a heart of endless gifts of love.

Your soul chant: I arrive with the energy of love wherever I am.

Your soul voice message: I am the bringer of love, the highest energy of all.

Your essence intention: to empower all with the capabilities of self-love.

LIFE PATH 7 – THE SPIRITUAL ONE

Your divine feminine sister energy: the messenger to the messengers

Your guidanceis to bring the realisation of spiritual empowerment to all.

Your divine feminine story: you have a voice of spirituality. You have a special resonance with the energy of spiritual love. It is tender and gentle and yet can instil strength and faith in others. You have the ability to create understanding where there was none before. You will inspire, teach and motivate through your words, gifts and strength. This is where you will find your own beautiful life fulfilment.

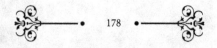

Your divine feminine gift: your fierce and unwavering love from a sometimes vulnerable heart enables you to share spiritual love with all.

Your soul chant: I am the essence of both spirit and earth.

Your soul voice message: to share divine and unending love, even where love has not yet reached.

Your essence intention: to both teach and reveal the magic of spiritual energy.

LIFE PATH 8 – THE MANIFESTER

Your divine feminine sister energy: the goddess of abundance.

Your guidance is to bring the understanding of the feminine and masculine energies of attraction.

Your divine feminine story: the magnetic energy of abundance has embraced you. You have the ability to create a true life of abundance for yourself. You have an energy of attraction. But it's important for you to realise that everything has to flow in harmony and balance. Your material world should be aligned with your spiritual world.

Your divine feminine gift: I am the energy of attraction.

Your soul chant: I live within the energy of abundance.

Your soul voice message: I am the energy of endless opportunities.

Your essence intention: to shine with the message there are endless possibilities of abundance for all.

LIFE PATH 9 – THE COMPASSIONATE HUMANITARIAN

Your divine feminine sister energy: the goddess of compassion.

Your guidance is to show the healing energies of forgiveness and compassion to all.

Your divine feminine story: yours is the shoulder that will

support others in times of trouble. You have a healing gift being a true listener and helping give others relief from their own burdens. You should though be more forgiving and less harsh with your own self.

You should listen to your own self with curiosity. This will help you overcome self-doubt and strengthen your ability to succeed! You have the power to transform your own sufferings into beautiful light!

Your divine feminine gift: I am the giver of kindness and compassion.

Your soul chant: I heal through releasing with forgiveness.

Your soul voice message: I am the word of compassion and kindness to the world.

Your essence intention: to bring the message of kindness and understanding to the world.

LIFE PATH 11 – THE ENLIGHTENED ONE

Your divine feminine sister energy: messenger of light

Your guidance is to know you are blessed and have the courage to follow your own path bravely.

Your divine feminine story: you are to be the leader of a journey of enlightenment for others. You will have the courage to share your light and knowledge with others. Be a motivator and inspiration to those that need your light and gifts. Helping others to see their own gifts within them will bring strength to your own light. In turn, this will help you create your own dream life.

Your divine feminine gift: I am gifted with knowledge and inspiration.

Your soul chant: I am blessed with the energy of enlightenment.

Your soul voice message: it is my soul mission to enlighten others to their own gifts and skills.

Your essence intention: to bring a sense of spirituality to all.

DIVINE FEMININE SISTER ENERGY JOURNALING TASK

Find which divine feminine sister energy you are by your life path number. How do you resonate with and share this energy?

_____

_____

_____

_____

_____

_____

_____

_____

_____

_____

_____

_____

_____

_____

_____

You

Let your eyes see what your soul feels.

So there you have it.
The KEY to working with universal magic.
But there's one thing left to tell you!
And that is…
YOU ARE THE MAGIC!
Your energy
Your inner beauty
Your inner child
Your truth
Your beautiful soul
Your gifts
Your skills
Your love
Your humour
Your laughter
 Your tears
Your generous heart
Your incredibility.
All that you shine!
You are what brings magic to the universe.
You are unique; there is no one else on this planet the same
as you!
You are blessed and you have blessings to give.
Let the energy and the magic flow through you as it was

always meant to do so. Step up, be brave, own your power and set a golden path for others to follow!

KNOW THAT YOU ARE DIVINELY LOVED.

KNOW THAT YOU ARE LOVE.

KNOW THAT YOU ARE THE KEY!

And finally for those of you who love a fairy story with a happy ending:

There was a young woman called Cinderella who was surrounded by negative people who told her she was worthless all the time. She was tired of her humdrum day to day life.

Then one day she said 'enough!' She understood that she did have the ability to have it all! She understood you don't have to carry other people's lies and ugliness around with you. She understood it doesn't matter who you are or where you're from, it's what's inside of you that counts. She understood the world is full of adventure and endless opportunities. She believed in the magic of the universe!

After one crazy night around the full moon, she took her glass slipper (the one she hadn't lost) and smashed through all her doubts and fears and followed her heart and dreams!

She ended up with a golden carriage, a fabulous dress, a cute date and a castle. She stepped up and became a queen!

All she did was believe in herself, let go of her fears and followed the magic!

Who's ready to start believing and step up?!

WE WERE ALL BORN TO LIVE IN LOVE, JOY AND ABUNDANCE.

And if you're looking for a fairy godmother I've got my wand ready!

Thank you!

Thank you for reading, we hope you enjoyed *The Key* by Denise Martinez Rossini.

Here's what you can do next:

Please leave a review on Amazon to let us know what you thought of the book.

Join Denise's group *Spiritual Queens Rising* on Facebook:
https://www.facebook.com/groups/spiritualqueensrising/

Sign up to the Tecassia newsletter to keep up to date on Denise Martinez Rossini's new releases:
https://tecassia.com/newsletter/

CPSIA information can be obtained
at www.ICGtesting.com
Printed in the USA
BVHW030518231020
591610BV00002BA/305